A book for all those concerned with teaching adults

TEACHING ON EQUAL TERMS

Edited by Jennifer Rogers

British Broadcasting Corporation

Published by the British Broadcasting Corporation
35 Marylebone High Street, London W1M 4AA

This publication accompanies the series
Teaching Adults *(first broadcast April–June 1968)*
repeated on BBC-2 on Thursdays at 7.00–7.30 p.m.
from 9 October to 11 December 1969

Printed in England by The Broadwater Press Ltd
Welwyn Garden City, Herts.

SBN: 563 08542 8

Cover photographs by permission of Radio Times Hulton Picture Library

Contents

INTRODUCTION
by Roger Owen

Roger Owen, producer of Teaching Adults, *a former teacher and BBC Education Officer, gives an individual perspective on the adult education world as he saw it when he made the series.*

Every time a BBC producer turns his hand to a new venture (or perhaps more properly I should say a BBC producer engaged as I am on adult educational programmes) he spends a period of three or four months 'working up' his subject. This period is sometimes known, a little portentously perhaps, as 'consultation', but in effect it simply means that he roams around talking to as many people in the given field as possible; keeping an eye open for likely contributors; testing the opinion of one expert against the comments of another; and, in the case of the series of programmes I worked on, observing as many situations as possible in which adults were being taught. It is from the background of this experience that I offer these comments. They are the views of an outsider, but those of an outsider who has had a unique chance to acquire an overview of the whole adult education world.

Producers also immerse themselves thoroughly in the literature of their subject – if any exists. There is in fact comparatively little good writing about adult teaching in Britain. It is true that there are some impressive accounts of the history of voluntary adult education; some frequently recondite bits of research on (say) the psycho-dynamics of group behaviour; some useful work on perhaps pro-grammed learning or the retraining of older workers. But there isn't a great deal of material which is of cash value to the practising teacher.

There is certainly nothing to equal in scale, volume and depth that

7

body of work which lies beneath the surface of any Education course at a good college of education. There *is* a body of knowledge about the way children should be taught, and in addition to this there exists an idea of the teacher as a 'practitioner' – as someone who learns the trade in actual practice, whose performance is observed and assessed and finally, from time to time, 'inspected'. There's a kind of professionalism in all this.

To a very large extent the teaching of adults in this country is in the hands of amateurs – in both the best and worst senses of that word. They are amateurs because although they love Photography or Car Maintenance, or Cake Decorating, their teaching of it is part-time, ill paid, and not central to their life's concerns. They are amateurs because although they were good craftsmen themselves, now that they are in the Training Department they rely on common sense, intuition and the way it's always been done. And even the Dons who know about Molecular Biology or Early Church Music are often amateurs too, because they sometimes regard teaching as an interference with the pursuit of truth, and discussion of method-ology as not quite the thing. That amongst all this, individual brilliance, dedication and heart exist, I've no doubt. In general, though, what is done is sanctioned by custom rather than enquiry. Good teachers exist because intelligent and sensitive *people* exist. Better teaching in general might appear if what is known about teaching were made more widely available – through courses, through training, perhaps even through books like this.

These are the possibly impertinent observations of an interested outsider. More authoritative comments follow in the book itself. For the rest, I will content myself with one or two of my strongest impressions after a six-month excursion into the field, and with one main proposition. First, the impressions.

I was often told that in the field of voluntary adult education, particularly that part under L.E.A. control, was to be found the *worst* teaching. After all, it was contended, here the part-timer, often untrained, predominated. Here were people with special skills in Millinery or Car Maintenance or Cake Decorating or French, but with 'no idea of putting it over'. And even when they *were* trained they carried over too uncritically the methods appropriate to the teaching of children.

Well, there might be something in this. I saw a good deal that was amiss in the Evening Institute field. Too many classes in which purposes were not defined; too much variety in the level of ability, experience, and achievement within single groups (a problem for the organisers, this); and too many classes in which the 'social and affiliative purposes' – as one bit of educational jargon puts it – of adult education got the better of everything else, i.e. everybody had a nice time but didn't learn much. There were classrooms, too, where teachers made all the classic mistakes which all of us have made. They talked too much; they tried to get a quart into a pint pot; they moved on too quickly before what they had taught had been assimilated. But on the whole my impressions were not too gloomy. I saw people enjoying themselves and I saw people learning, and as a proof that learning had taken place, I saw them carrying away bits of good pottery, or occasional tables, or a nicely upholstered chair, or a competent oil painting.

I don't think any of these recreative skills need be despised and I *do* think that the occasions on which they are practised would be educationally more significant if questions of task and judgement were sometimes explored. But there is something dangerous in the view which I have heard propounded which says, in effect, that in themselves these are really low-order skills. This is the view which says Dressmaking should lead to Design which will bring us to Art, or 'via Continental Cooking for Beginners to the Italian Renaissance'. There's snobbery here. In other words I think questions of value should be allowed to arise, and not be insisted on.

In fact it was in these subjects where questions of value are most explicitly dealt with that I felt my severest anxieties – in literature, psychology, philosophy, art appreciation, for example; the provinces in fact of the University Extra-Mural Departments and the Workers' Educational Association. Here I saw much that was heartwarming, and touching, because to see people 'coming' to things which were destroyed for them at bad schools or to which they were never given a chance to come, is a moving experience. But there are problems. First of all there is the frequently sporadic approach to written work which several of the authors of these chapters comment on. If people are pursuing a demanding intellectual discipline, then the teacher needs to know how well they are doing, and if one of the agreed conventions of the game is that nobody is obliged to do written work, then the teacher has great difficulty in doing this. And unlike his colleagues in the schools, the Extra-Mural tutor is not even exposed to the crude accountability of an examination system. In the kind of situation I have described, there is often no verification that learning has taken place at all – not a coffee table, not a flower arrangement, not a decorated cake.

And now the proposition. The more I thought about adult teaching the less inclined I was to see it as a category. Let me list some of the points that were made to me about the *distinctive* characteristics of adult teaching. I was told that adults don't learn unless they feel *confident* and that early failure inhibits further learning. Well, every good infant teacher knows that that's true of children. I was told that an adult teacher must treat his class as *individuals*. That's a counsel of perfection for *all* teachers. The widely differing back-grounds of the people in an adult class were emphasised for me. In the modern primary school the breakdown of streaming by ability has led to an increase in individual teaching, and to work centred on individual interest. In other words adults are no more and no less individual than children. I was told that a voluntary adult class can vote with its feet – the teacher hadn't got a captive audience. Children vote by not learning and it's a poor teacher who mistakes silent acquiescence based on the legal sanctions of the Education Act for the real thing. I was told that you mustn't talk down to adults. I've never heard anyone enjoining a teacher to talk down to *children*.

Finally I was told by Eunice and Meredith Belbin (whose research on adult learning is perhaps the most relevant we have) that adults prefer *learning* to being taught: that what they find out for them-selves is retained far better than what they learn by being 'told'. This is a truism in Primary education – almost a cliché.

There are obvious differences between adults and children as learners. No adult teacher is *in loco parentis*; older people in general (though not in particular) have poorer short-term memories, less visual acuity and, at the end of the day, are probably more tired. Essentially it seems to me, though, that whatever actually happens in the classrooms and lecture rooms, it would be for the good if the common currency of educational thinking in relation to children was circulated more widely in what is not so fundamentally a different world.

WHAT DO THEY EXPECT?
by H. A. Jones

The students themselves must be at the core of any study of adult teaching and learning. In this chapter, Professor Henry Arthur Jones, Vaughan Professor of Education at the University of Leicester and previously Principal of the City Literary Institute, London, looks at some of the motives which bring adults of all sorts back into the classroom, and discusses what the characteristics of the adult class are.

There can be learning without a teacher but there can't be teaching without a learner. However important the quality of teaching – and the whole of teacher-training would be nothing but prodigal waste if quality of teaching was not important – it is still true that in the end there is no such thing as teaching. There is only learning, and it is the students who do it. All the teacher can do is to stimulate the urge to learn, facilitate the learning, and then show what has been learnt. In the current jargon the teacher simply manages the learning situation.

But this is really too simple. When Grandpa, standing proudly beside the most pneumatic onions or the spikiest gladioli in the Show, says, 'Look what I've grown', he is making an absurdly arrogant claim. He cannot *grow* anything; the life urge of vegetation is not his to command. Yet it is still his name that we put on the prize-winner's card, rather than 'God', or 'The Life-Force', or 'Nature'. For what he can do is to go along with nature, observing and understanding, creating conditions that will lead to the results that his observation has led him to expect.

Teaching is much like this, a patient process of watching for the moment at which change becomes perceptible and then applying skill to hasten the change. It calls for some special qualities and much special knowledge in the teacher, but it *depends* on the qualities of the learner. Any discussion of adult teaching must begin with him.

What is he like ? Up to a few years ago it would have been easy to answer this question by saying that he would be lower middle class in background, educated in some way beyond the minimum school-leaving age, probably in his late thirties or forties, more likely to be a woman than a man, and to be found in a non-vocational evening class run by a Responsible Body (that is, a university or the Workers' Educational Association) or at an evening institute. This has now changed. Adult students are to be found in a great diversity of contexts, doing many different things, and at whatever point we come in to teach them we need to be aware of this range.

In the first place the old assumption that vocational education took place in youth and that adult education was non-vocational has been undermined by social and technological change. Few people nowadays can expect to remain long in a job without being involved in some sort of retraining. This is as true of managers and magistrates as of process workers and policemen. Everyone who has taken professional qualifications finds them being steadily outdated by new discoveries. Then day-release education is no longer restricted to the young worker. Increasing numbers of trade unionists, and especially shop stewards, attend day-release courses in industrial studies, and pre-retirement courses are often arranged in this form too. The changes in social services not only involve further training for those already employed but also open up new opportunities for men and women to train in adult life. The full-time housewife receives her occupational retraining at the local evening institute and may be doing so in the morning or afternoon instead of the evening. Finally there are those wives who, having married early in the modern way and seen their family grow up, are still young enough to contemplate a new career and to train for it. Many of these need basic qualifications like O-levels, as well as the habits of study, and they look to adult classes for help. Learning in a formal sense now goes on throughout life in a way that has never happened before and education is being seen not as a commodity to be obtained for the children but as the basis for consolidating a position in life or as the gateway to wider opportunities.

Adult students in all these different kinds of activity will display certain characteristics and expectations. As will appear in later chapters, the whole range of adult education can be considered as a single field simply by virtue of the fact that the students are adults. This implies consent, even when attendance appears not to be voluntary, as in industrial training, a point we shall come back to later. These general characteristics, however, are nearer the surface in the voluntary, non-vocational type of class and I shall therefore describe them mainly in that context. They are equally relevant in all other contexts where the students are adult.

The usual word in German for a member of an adult class is *Hörer*, 'listener'. In the English-speaking world we don't like this apparently passive concept and we call him a 'student'. The word is derived from Latin and means 'showing zeal or eagerness', though it goes back to an older root meaning 'going or rushing forth'. Root meanings are often illuminating. The primary quality of the adult learner is that he must go (if not rush) forth, and since his class will traditionally take place on a winter's evening when the counter-pull of home and fireside are strongest, he must have some reason for doing so. We call this his motivation and (frankly) we don't know much about it.

At a superficial level to ask the students why they have come and to get an answer is not very difficult. A group of teachers in a course of mine, mainly teachers of crafts, tried this recently on their students and found that, whilst they got a variety of reasons from the men, the women replied, almost without exception, 'to get away from home'. Here were people for whom home and fireside had no counter-pull, even on a wet night. Now, over the whole country and the whole range of subjects, two out of every three adult students are women. It looks as though the weekly class is the British housewife's release from the bondage of cooker, duster and needle. But as likely as not she joins a class in Cookery, Dressmaking, Soft Furnishing or Flower Arranging and spends her evening on the very things she is supposed to be escaping.

Moreover it was found that over a third of the women who said they wanted to get away from home were in fact at work during the day, if only part-time. Clearly the attraction of the class was not simply to find a change from home chores: the motive was much more complex, having to do with a need to understand and perfect those tasks that were being left behind. Part of it would be social, the wish to meet other people in a context of familiar concerns; but might it not be much more than this? Did these women perhaps feel less guilty at being away from home if their avowed purpose was to learn the domestic arts? Was it that they felt home-making to be their true profession, whether they had another job or not, and found the readiest path to self-fulfilment through learning to tackle it in a professional way? Or was it simply that, feeling permanently on the brink of not coping any more, they were just appealing for help? A simple question about why they joined the class cannot explore these depths. In the answers they gave, these women were not describing a motive so much as a satisfaction they found when there.

A few years ago, at the City Literary Institute, I became interested in the relatively large number of people who applied for the beginners' class in Classical Greek. This is a difficult subject, especially for adults with limited time, but there were always more applicants than we could accommodate in one class, and I arranged to interview them all at enrolment-time to find out what brought them. A few had done some Greek at schools and wanted to brush it up; a few had returned from holidays in Greece fired with zeal to read the ancient tongue; but by far the greatest number were not really concerned with *Greek* at all. They appeared to believe that Greek was the especial mark of the fully educated person and what they wanted was – not a certificate to say they were educated – but a chance to try themselves out against this standard to see if they could reach it. It was an objective test like a four-minute mile. But why the need to prove this to themselves anyway? (The fact that few continued beyond the first year is understandable: they had discovered what they needed to know, that they either could learn Greek or they couldn't.)

It will be seen then that the *motive to attend* may be quite different from the *motive to learn*, and that what students are really wanting to learn may be something unconnected with the chosen subject, something about themselves. And whether they come with that conscious intention or not, they will, if the teacher knows his job, learn a great deal about themselves, their limitations and capacities. Adult education is a voyage of self-discovery.

I have said that we do not know much about students' motives: I do not think they matter much. The teacher faced with a class of mixed standards and interests has no time for depth-analysis of motivation. What is much more pertinent is the student's self-concept in the class, that is, the picture he has in his own mind of what he is doing there, what he expects of the teacher, of the subject, and of the other students, and how he relates his attendance at the class with all his other concerns, desires and responsibilities. This is the level at which the teacher will meet him. It can perhaps be best approached by way of four generally held expectations about the educational process.

First, the students will expect to be taught. This is not quite so simple or so self-evident as it may seem, for what it means is that they expect the teacher to do the active work while they sit back (like the German *Hörer*) and wait for his magic to transform them. We are all to a large extent prisoners of our earlier educational experience and at school we were led to believe that it was the teacher who made us learn. The older our students now, the more deeply will their educational expectations be rooted in old-fashioned, rigid but forceful teaching methods. The most exciting of new methods, especially discovery methods where the teacher seems to withdraw from activity, may well meet a blank wall of incomprehension in such students: they may go on week after week waiting for the teaching to *start*, and may eventually drop out of the class convinced that nothing has yet happened.

Classes in creative writing sometimes exhibit this characteristic in an acute form. At the first meeting the students will readily agree with the tutor that what they need is to practise the craft of writing in various forms, to study the works of masters ancient and modern, and to cultivate their individual vision into the heart of human experience; and some of them will believe it. But the rest will qualify all this with a private reservation: what they expect is that the teacher will eventually disclose to them the magic formula for publishable stories in women's magazines. It would be unreasonable to expect him to do this the first week, so they dutifully (but no more than dutifully) carry out the teacher's exercises, playing him along until the moment of revelation shall arrive. But there is no magic formula, and the end is disappointment because the students' misguided expectation has prevented any real learning from taking place. In a similar fashion many people in language classes will expect to be taught in the formal mode of their schooldays, based on the recitation of memorised rules to the teacher; and students of art will feel cheated if the laws of perspective are not enacted at the outset.

I am not saying that expectations of this kind are right or that we must give way to them. In planning our work as teachers, however, in exploring the new methods, new ideas and new equipment now becoming accessible in many subjects, we need to be aware of the revolution in attitudes that we may be demanding of our students, who will generally have grown up with the belief that teaching means making them learn.

The second of the four expectations is linked with the first. It is that the teacher will display an appropriate professionalism. He will be expected to establish that he himself can do whatever it is that he teaches, and do it well. He may also show that he knows something about teaching, but in this matter much will be forgiven him if he clearly knows his stuff. Indeed, since it is said that those who can, do, and those who cannot, teach, perhaps it may seem that those who are no good at teaching are the best practitioners and their prestige may rise accordingly.

What a mistake this is. Of course the teacher needs to be competent in his subject, but he is being employed as a teacher and teaching is his true art. The danger is that the skilled practitioner of an art or craft who is no teacher will be led by his students' expectations to turn his class into an audience for his performances or demonstrations. However delightful the resulting experience the situation is not a learning situation. The effect of the teacher's skill is not to lead the students to the frontiers of their ability so that they discover they can do things they never dreamt of attempting: it may simply reinforce their suspicion that they will never be any good and they might as well not bother to try.

The escape from this danger lies in the third of these expectations of students, which is that they will be made to work. This may appear to run counter to popular belief among teachers of adults, who think that because the students come voluntarily they must not be taxed too heavily or they will stay away. This is a myth that has no foundation. Just as students expect to be taught, they expect that the teacher will make demands on them: in their earlier experience the worthwhile teacher always did. Students do not resist demands for hard work until they have been taught to do so by the apologetic attitude of teachers.

There are many evidences of this expectation. In a survey of dropouts from adult classes in 1966 it was found that more students dropped out because the class made too few demands on them, especially in the matter of homework, than because the demands were too heavy. The teachers who command the most loyal and regular attendance are invariably those who press their students hard, for the students realise that there is much to be gained by being present and much to be lost by being away. There is now an impressive number of classes who have carried through projects and published the results. The most obvious fields are in archaeology and local history, but aspects of local sociology, social welfare, planning and architecture have also appeared more recently. Anyone who has taken part in such an experiment will be aware of the prodigious amount of work demanded of the students, as also of the cheerfulness and sincerity with which it is done.

Years ago, among tutors of University Tutorial Classes (in which the official regulations required 'written work' to be done by all students and the register had a space for the tutor's certificate that it had been done) there used to be energetic discussion about 'how to get written work out of students'. The very phrase is indicative of a sense of defeat. Yet many such classes produced frequent and good essays from a majority of the members simply because the tutor assumed without question that the students were ready to read and write regularly at home: for so they were.

It is perhaps in those crafts like Dressmaking and Woodwork where a specific product is made that the problems arise most clearly in this connection. One often hears of people in dressmaking classes who have joined simply to receive expert help in making up a pattern they have already bought and who resist all attempts by the teacher to teach. I have no doubt of their existence, but I cannot help wondering how many of them have been reinforced in their original thought by teachers like the Misses Kerr in *The Prime of Miss Jean Brodie* who 'were incapable of imparting any information. . . Instead of teaching sewing they took each girl's work in hand, one by one, and did most of it for her. In the worst cases they unstitched what had been done and did it again, saying, "This'll not do".' However urgent the student's desire for a dress or a coffee-table the very fact that he has joined a class reveals something of his attitude to education, and given the right sense of relevance about his work in the class there is every likelihood that he will find the broad and systematic exploration of the subject more rewarding than the mere production of an article. His expectation that he will be made to work can be harnessed at the outset, or it can be stifled into passivity.

At this point, however, we come to the fourth of these expectations, which is the complement of the third. However much students may expect to be called on to work, and however well they respond to the demand, they also expect to be treated with due dignity. They are far more vulnerable than students in any other context: criticism that strikes harshly, a patronising tone, humiliation of any kind, or plain neglect can all wound deeply and the teacher who is not sensitive to the sensitivities of his students will soon have no students. Holding this balance between encouragement and correction, so that criticism is accepted as constructive and progress is felt to be there throughout, is one of the teacher's most delicate tasks.

This expectation derives from the fact that the students are adult: that is, they have been earning a living, managing a home and an income, holding down a job and so on, for a long time. They are the equal of the teacher, if not his superior, in all respects but the knowledge of the subject they have come to acquire. The point was made as long ago as 1855 by Frederick Denison Maurice, founder of the Working Men's College, who wrote (in *Learning and Working*), 'a man has rights, has a knowledge, has a position, which must be taken for granted, and respected; that he must under no circumstances be put on a first form, and turned into a child. You cannot do it; you have no business to attempt it. The world has been teaching him – I must add with all reverence, God has been teaching him – whatever you have been doing.'

Two facts about the adult qualities of students can be mentioned in particular. The first is that everyone is short of time: merely rearranging one's life so as to allow a regular weekly attendance is not usually easy. The research into dropouts showed that over 70% of them were the victims of external circumstances that had nothing to do with the class – illness of self or family, change of job or address, problems at home; and also it confirmed that a number of students who did not drop out had had to face similar crises. When so many of our students are liable to meet such conflicting claims on their time they cannot be expected to give high priority to the class unless they feel, not only that it is important to them, but that they are important to it. Students will often arrive at the class full of conscious virtue at the difficulties they have had to surmount in order to be there at all. We as teachers have little inkling of this, perhaps fortunately, but our whole relationship with them must be one that accepts and engages the adult dignity deriving from all the other roles they fill in their daily lives.

The other point is that, delicate though this relationship is, it enjoys the great advantage of the students' broad experience of life. Adult education is sometimes charged with being too bourgeois, and it may be true that the lower-paid industrial workers are underrepresented, especially in the evening institutes. Even there, however, the members of any group will be only superficially alike. Collectively they will span a great range of experience and activities, all of which may at times be brought into the focus of the class work. This is what is meant by 'extending the subject', dealt with in full by George Whittle in Chapter 7. Because of the collective wisdom of the class – whether the wisdom that finds answers or the wisdom that probes and forms questions – the class work can be brought constantly into the realm of values and the main issues of life, where the charge of triviality which is sometimes levelled at adult classes cannot possibly be sustained. To exploit this wisdom, however, the teacher needs to know the students, to see them all in the context of their lives outside the class, and to be able to recognise the moment at which he should draw back and let the unique experience of a student fill the stage.

It is by this route, by the recognition of the adult quality of his students, that the alert teacher finds his way out of a difficulty that many teachers complain of, namely the mixture of abilities to be found in a single class. Teachers of languages appear to suffer most (or complain most) about this, for there are not only administrative problems like the insufficiency of numbers at each level of ability to sustain a separate class; there is also the unwillingness of many students to believe they have really learnt enough to progress to the next stage. (I have known French Beginners who have gone on beginning for years on end.) But even in languages classes it is possible to establish an atmosphere of corporate purpose in which the more advanced students help the others along, not by exhibiting their superior ability but by contributing to the common process of learning that is felt by all to be going on. If the teacher thinks of the students as simply a set of receptacles into which he is to decant a measure of his precious subject he is bound to find their different capacities a problem. If he sees them as a group of human beings, each one a different window on the wide world outside, each with a distinctive kind of contribution to make to the interaction of the group with the subject-matter, and each one capable of his own particular insight into the learning problems involved, he will see their mixture of abilities as one of his greatest advantages. Of course they will differ in their knowledge of the subject; of course they will learn at differing rates and in differing ways; of course they will fasten on different aspects of the subject as important because of the complexity of the motivation that brought them to the class; but out of all this the teacher who knows his students as well as his subject can fashion a learning group that is stimulating for its very diversity.

Whether or not the teacher chooses to bring this diversity into play the students will do so for themselves. Discussion during the coffee break may derive from the class work but it soon ranges far beyond, for the students are now relating to one another as people: they are freer to do so when the situation is informal. But they are also reacting to one another as people when the class is in progress, even if they are sitting in silent attention. It is easy for the teacher to believe that he is engaged in a simple two-way traffic with each student individually; he looks round the class and sees pairs of eyes fixed on him or intent on their work, and when a student speaks it is often a direct question to the teacher. What the teacher doesn't hear is the interior monologue going on in the head of each student, in which responses to the teacher's words and to all the other students mix in with recollections of other experiences, some perversely irrelevant, and which forms the sound-track of his learning. I would recommend every teacher of adults to look back from time to time at two or three pages of James Joyce's *Ulysses* where Bloom stands by the graveside at Paddy Dignam's funeral: as he listens to the words of the priest his attention alternates between genuine sorrow for his dead friend and reactions to the other mourners ('Now who is that lanky-looking galoot in the mackintosh?') in a way that is very like what goes on in our students' heads as we try to engage them in learning. A salutary reminder of all this was furnished by the research into dropouts that has already been mentioned. Of those who left because of dissatisfaction with the class there were as many who did so because they didn't like other students as because they disliked the teacher.

The general expectations I have been describing do not apply only to students in non-vocational classes. They will appear in all the great range of educational situations that can now be met with in adult life, for they are expectations about the nature of the educational experience. Nevertheless they will also be modified by each successive experience of the process. For example, the trade unionist who has attended a day-release course and the executive who has been on a senior management course will have acquired techniques for identifying and analysing problems, and for distinguishing between fact and opinion; the worker who has been taught a new operation by modern methods of industrial training will have seen for himself how a complex process can be broken down into logical steps and mastered by easy stages; the housewife studying for her O-levels will have rediscovered the rewards of hard work, the limitations of formal teaching and the frustrations of home study; the learner of a foreign language who has followed a broadcast series will have found that learning can be much closer to entertainment than was ever apparent in the curriculum of his schooldays. These educational experiences are nowadays all part of that total area of adult experience that the teacher can mobilise for the benefit of the class.

All who have worked in these fields are familiar with the rewards and the excitement of teaching adults and we may sometimes be too ready to see therein a self-evident justification for our work. By concentrating our attention on our students, however, by responding to their expectations and exploiting their breadth of experience, by involving them in a group process of learning that engages them as whole people, and by reminding ourselves that it is always their learning and not our teaching (or even our learning) that is the justification, we can ensure that they too share the rewards and the excitement.

Further reading

GLYNN, D. R. and JONES, H. A. Student wastage in *Adult Education* Sept. 1967, pp. 139–49.

TRENAMAN, J. Education in the adult population in *Adult Education* Winter 1957, pp. 216–24, and March 1962, pp. 303–11 (reprint).

ROBINSON, J. Exploring adult interests in *Adult Education* May 1965, pp. 27–35.

VERNER, C. and BOOTH, A. *Adult education* New York: Centre for Applied Research in Education, 1964. Chap. 2 The adult.

JAMES, W. What makes adults learn? in *Teaching Adults* October 1967.

CLEUGH, M. F. *Educating older people* Tavistock P., 1962.

JOYCE, J. *Ulysses* Penguin, 1969, pp. 110–12.

HOW DO THEY LEARN?
by R. M. Belbin

A great deal of research has now been done in Britain on how adults differ from children when they have something new to learn. Here, Dr R. M. Belbin, himself a leading researcher on learning and retraining, discusses problems of memory, ageing, and intelligence in adults and suggests what types of learning are most easily accomplished by adults. In particular, he describes the 'discovery' method which he believes to be the most appropriate to the needs of the adult learner. Dr Belbin is an industrial and research consultant.

Types of learning

It is quite a common belief that as we age we lose the ability to learn. People probably think of one form of learning ability that declines and suppose that this is representative of a loss of learning ability in general. This is an error we must avoid. Research now indicates that learning takes different forms and that while one form may show signs of deterioration, another is well maintained, especially if given plenty of opportunity for exercise. Adults certainly need to learn if they are to maintain a fair adjustment to their environment and good relationships with people with whom they associate. Only in senility does learning break down completely. Then the individual becomes entirely dependent on what he has *previously* learned.

Let us start by looking at the principal modes of learning and at their significance at different periods of life. The main form of learning in infancy and very early childhood is by imitation. In many ways a young child may be likened to a high-speed copying machine. Everything is copied, the language of the parent, the behaviour, the attitudes, even the mannerisms. The young child is a wonderful mimic even to the point of high comedy.

Memorising is the next form of learning we encounter. The nursery rhyme figures well before the child starts school. Meaning tends to be of secondary account. The child may persist for a long time saying

'Harold be thy name . . .' in place of 'Hallowed be thy name . . .'. The valueless is assimilated as well as the useful. I still retain a certain fluency in remembering from school the Latin for 'O table!' and 'about to be loved' or the Greek for 'you are being loosed'. The celebrated French sentence 'Voici la plume de ma tante' rings in my ears, although I have never had occasion to seek the missing pen of my aunt in France nor to proclaim the fact.

Memorising is really a sophisticated form of imitation aimed at reproducing spoken or written tracts. It has its value because human society is so deeply involved with language. Before the advent of literacy the transmission of culture depended almost completely on human memory. Medicine, law and history could cover no greater span than that which could be remembered. It is no wonder that a good memory traditionally held such a valued place in education. In bygone days the bard would be expected to be word perfect in the two great works of Homer, the Iliad and the Odyssey, each comprising 24 books. Only in the last century has the great need for memorising been over-come by universal literacy and the availability of documentary aids – the manual, the chart, the textbook and the timetable.

We now come to a third important type of learning ability – dis-covering. If human society just rested on the abilities of its members to imitate and memorise, it would never be able to advance, to renew itself, to conquer fresh fields. The youngest children explore their own physical capacities and the material world of their environment, but this is partly held in check by the tendency to imitate so that the cautious and the challenging ways of learning are nicely counter-balanced. This balance is changed as childhood passes and the adult personality achieves maturity through independence and self-reliance.

Since adults are less ready to learn through imitating it can be seen that research and exploration gain added importance for them. Dis-covery becomes the typical form of adult learning. We see it regularly in the factory. Faced with the task of operating a machine that has been newly introduced in a department the adult likes to find out all about it for himself, in contrast to the school-leaver who is much readier to learn by following the demonstrations and heeding the words of an instructor. The adult can still learn that way, but it is not usually the way he wishes to learn.

Education ends for many people in their mid teens after which they enter into occupations that offer very short periods of training before settling down into a routine form of life. Hence, it might be said that some never really experience the advantages of adult learning. They may only recognise that they have lost the capacity for childhood learning.

The teacher's response to adult needs

Educationists responsible for teaching adults may develop remarkable skill in adapting their methods to a class, sometimes intuitively without perhaps realising what they are doing and why. I certainly admired the skill, fluency and expertise of some of the professional teachers who were shown in the 'Teaching Adults' series. But Sarah Kent, the young art teacher who appeared in programmes 4 and 10, deserves special mention. Her presentation really took into account what the adult demands when he learns. She was dealing with a dangerous subject – Art. The glimpses we were shown were confined – even more dangerous – to geometric forms, relationships and symbols. What a subject for controversy! Clearly she had thought out her own views, for there was every sign that the lesson had been well prepared, but they were never imposed. The class members were introduced to problems and questions about their reactions. Miss Kent did not assert that abstract figures are capable of exciting emotions according to their shape and position on a blank sheet of paper. It was through the contributions of class members that 'discoveries' were made: that emotions vary according to where the shape is placed on the paper and that these emotions are shared by us all.

Sarah Kent's easy style can be deceptive. It looked as though the teacher was rather incidental to the class; as though it was a good class that just arrived somewhere under its own steam; that the BBC's cameraman was in luck the day he called. The expert always makes a job look just too easy. But the prospective teacher of adults will realise the difficulty when in preparing his teaching programme he has to reconcile the freedom which an adult demands in his learning with the need to cover a certain amount of material in a limited amount of time.

This need will be further appreciated in relation to our own experiment in teaching principles of electricity to trainee drivers of diesel electric trains. Electricity is not like Art; it does not offer personal scope for expression and interpretation. There is a *correct* answer to each problem. The principles are immutable. How then can a training programme be devised to allow an adult to develop his own answers through exploration? The answer seems to lie in preparing challenging problems and presenting them in a series which enables the trainee to build up his own concepts. But since each individual's experience is different, since his powers of comprehension vary, since he can fall into error or become bogged down, a programme on its own is insufficient. It needs to be supported by a teacher who can allocate tasks according to an indivdual's progress and capabilities and monitor the results. This type of teacher doesn't appear to be teaching, any more than did Sarah Kent. Someone who is teaching adults a technical subject may look from the outside much more like a consultant than a teacher.

The scope of the discovery method

The Discovery method* – a method we advocate as useful for teaching adults – aims to find a means of presenting tasks and problems in an arrangement which allows trainees to find out relationships and concepts for themselves. This is the method which we have been using experimentally for some years. More recently we have conducted experiments in four countries; the United Kingdom, Austria, Sweden and the United States. The results indicate that this method of training is not only preferred but is more effective than traditional methods, if judged by the ability to *apply* what has been learned; that is, to use what has been learned in some new setting. There is also some indication that the method is relatively more effective with older adults.

Our television illustration of the Discovery method was taken from the teaching of chess. As far as I was concerned it would have been much easier simply to have told my would-be player how the King and Rook moved and how to make a checkmate. But the adult player doesn't like sitting there being told. Is it likely that he would wait to hear about the Knight, the Queen, the Bishop and the Pawn and all the complicated laws governing castling and Pawns taken *en passant*? Adults are inclined to 'switch off' or to allow some small phrase to claim their attention, which they will enlarge upon and tie up with their own personal experience while the teacher goes on unheard.

We still have to explain why adults are almost as reluctant to learn from a book. A book of instructions is a logical (if less satisfying) way of learning how to proceed. But the problem of responding to a large

* For further information see *The Discovery Method: an international experiment in retraining*, by R. M. Belbin, O.E.C.D. publications, Paris, 1969.

amount of written instructions is akin to listening to a lot of spoken instructions in that there are many bits of information that only make sense when the end is reached. So all these bits of information have to be *remembered* over this interval.

Those who learn by discovery seem in contrast to be singularly free from failure both of attention and of retention. He who discovers how a chess piece moves tends to remember it well, due perhaps to the fact that he can more easily reconstruct the experience which led him to the right conclusion.

*Applying the discovery method to chess**

Four minutes or so of viewing is barely sufficient to give an overall picture of the Discovery method in action in the teaching of chess. Perhaps it was just sufficient to bring out how very early the learner can accomplish a *whole* task. You will recollect that in the first stage the pupil distinguished and named (unaided) the King and the Rook. Next the moves of these pieces were 'discovered'. The task was arranged in such a way that I spent more time saying 'Yes, that's right' than 'No, that's wrong'. After that we reached the big task of trying to *checkmate* the King (i.e. so he couldn't move without being taken) with two Rooks in action together. To get that far ought to take about five minutes. If the learner succeeds without too much help or hinting, he will have grasped the whole object of the exercise through his own efforts.

This is the turning-point, for most of what is learned thereafter is simply the development of technique for reaching the same goal. Our next exercise would consist of a King and a Rook versus a King, obviously more difficult than checkmating with a King and two Rooks. Then we progress to checkmating with a King and Queen (so learning about the dangers of an 'accidental draw' through *stale-mating*). And having learned in the process about the moves the Queen makes we are all set for the next task. This is the White King and all the White Pawns versus the Black King and all the Black Pawns. When the Pawn advances up its file and reaches the end of the board it is 'converted' into a Queen. This powerful potentate then has a fine frolic round the board swiping all the opposing Pawns. The first player to gain a Queen under these conditions usually wins and further practice is gained in *checkmating*. There is no point in

* In Programme 3 of 'Teaching Adults', Dr Belbin demonstrated how the Discovery Method could be used to teach chess to a complete beginner.

teaching that a Queen is a more powerful piece than any other. The players soon realise the relative value of pieces by the experience in completing the tasks. Nor is there any point in teaching the value of *combinations*. It will soon emerge that when the King supports his forward Pawns there is more chance of gaining a Queen. The art of training is to know what to leave out so we are able to rush on to chess strategy. A few carefully chosen tasks will enable us to recognise the nature of a *sacrifice*, a *gambit*, a *pin*, and a *discovered threat*. This is the very meat of chess.

Teaching something complex like chess to mature adults (usually regarded as poor beginners) is an instructive lesson to teachers themselves. Even the sophisticated teacher falls into traps. When practising on a 'guinea-pig' adult just before the live filming on an absolute novice, I was impressed with how easily the middle-aged woman I was instructing was upset and disturbed by the committing of error and by having this pointed out to her. The task set needs to be judged to a nicety. If the task is not right for the level of development of understanding reached we cannot compensate by putting more effort into our teaching. This tends to drive the teacher and pupil alike to frenzy. It is better to switch to a new task and to maintain our theme of continuous achievement.

Throughout all our tasks one thing stands out: how carefully we keep away from *explanation* and from any attempt to demand that our trainee *remembers* what we are teaching. Paradoxically, adults understand better when we refrain from explanation (they like to explain it to themselves) and they remember better when they are free from the strain of memorising.

Problems of memory in learning

Our reluctance to stress the need to remember requires some elaboration. A loss in the capacity of memory can underlie a great deal of failure in learning and so indicates that simple memorising is not a reliable basis upon which learning should be founded. Yet contrary to common belief the ability to memorise does not decline very much with age amongst healthy individuals given *ideal* conditions: for example, in the case of short-term memory span, people in their twenties and fifties can hear and repeat about the same number of digits, usually not more than eight. Try it with some imaginary telephone numbers. As the digit-span increases we forget or fall into error. So our short-term memory has a very limited capacity.

Scientists have formulated the notion that during this period of short-term storage we are in reality scanning the information input to find a way of processing it for long-term storage. It is then encoded in a form enabling it to be retrieved, decoded and reconstructed at some future date. This may sound highly conjectural. But something like this probably occurs if we take account of what we know of the physiology of the central nervous system and the brain which is capable of working only in limited ways and certainly cannot operate like a photographic plate. This short-term storage period during which the scanning takes place is therefore rather critical. Subjectively it may be experienced as an attempt to find meaning (which neurologically allows it to be 'encoded').

Now what we do know for certainty is that as we age the efficiency of short-term memory is easily impaired by any other activities that take place during the periods when bits of information are being temporarily held. For example, older people have been shown to lose their digit span more easily than younger people if during the period between hearing and repeating a number they have to write down certain letters of the alphabet. Any activity it seems, during this critical period *interferes* with the process by which we memorise. This will explain the ease with which a telephone number is forgotten while the subscriber is looking up the STD code. There are a good many other types of difficulty which adults encounter during learning but many of these difficulties can be overcome by changing the teaching method. Some guides on how to do this have been summarised by us in the Industrial Training Research Unit and are given at the end of Dr Martin's chapter.

Education, experience and the individual

One limitation in any general set of principles is that people vary. What is more, it seems that the extent of this variation increases as we age. In A. T. Welford's celebrated book *Ageing and Human Skill* the differences between people in measures of skilled performance on experimental tasks were shown to widen in each succeeding age group. Some older people completed the experimental tasks with a measure of proficiency that was comparable to the average performance of people in their twenties. But the worse performers were usually a fair bit worse than the worst of each of the younger age groups.

Individual differences are also very important in terms of knowledge. The more people know the more there is to build on. But equally more energy has to be spent in overcoming what has been learned if it is not altogether appropriate. The problem here is what is termed 'unlearning'. The story that I tried to tell in the programme to illustrate this (but cut short for fear of overrunning our time) related to the company of brewers which withdrew horse-drawn service vehicles for replacement by motor vehicles. 283 displaced drivers covering a wide age span were then trained to drive motor vehicles and their results could be compared with people of the same age from outside the company that had not had this experience with dray-horses. The evidence showed that up to the age of 40 previous experience in driving horse-drawn vehicles was an advantage in passing the test, but after the age of 40 people with no experience did better than those *with* experience.

It is education which usually offers benefits in overcoming 'unlearning'. To express this more positively, education facilitates the ability to learn, and continuing education reduces the dependence on what has been previously learned. For example, one study of mature adults attending a teachers' training course showed that those who, since their formal education ceased, had been members of other courses achieved better examination results than those who had not. Another comparable result was shown in a recent nation-wide study of persons undergoing a course of training for a Coal Preparation Certificate. The examination consisted of both practical and theoretical sections. A personal questionnaire was filled in by the trainees and from this it emerged that while many had engaged in no form of educational activity since leaving school, some had taken an interest in other activities involving learning, attending courses on musical appreciation, trade union affairs and so on. On the practical examination there was no difference between the two groups, indicating that the groups in general ability and experience were comparable, but on the theoretical section of the examination the 'experienced learners' achieved appreciably better results than the others, although the type of learning upon which they had been engaged had no obvious relevance to the examination.

Besides the general advantage which education confers there are also specific advantages. Much depends in learning on the degree of competence in such primary activities as reading, writing and arithmetic. Many problems in teaching adults have their roots in some basic educational deficiency which an individual may struggle to disguise. Our experience with training programmes in industry suggests these deficiencies may be far more common than is supposed. The teacher may fail to unearth them because they are so unexpected, especially when the learners are apparently keen and responsive. In teaching middle-aged workers to acquire new engineering skills, we have often linked poor workmanship with failure to measure accurately. It is not uncommon to find that some adults do not see the relationships between quarters, eighths and sixteenths of an inch. And when I asked several adult trainees how many sixteenths there were in an inch, one thought there were 10 and another 12. Others show uncertainty about *where* to start to measure when using a rule. Similar and quite remarkable stories could be quoted on literacy. The point that seems to emerge is that many an adult trainee has some blind-spot which he has long covered up by avoiding the situations in which his weakness is exposed.

One of the most important factors affecting individual progression in learning is intelligence. Where intelligence has a direct bearing on the nature of the learning that is undertaken, it is usual to find amongst a group of adults in a class that variations in intelligence are more closely related to the results achieved than the variations in age. What is less commonly realised is that personality too is a major variable. In some recent experiments in the learning ability of adults all the subjects took intelligence and personality tests; the latter measuring introversion-extroversion (how withdrawn people are) and stability-neuroticism (their tendency to anxiety). In one task involving learning to read a micrometer, individual differences in results were more closely linked with measurable personality differences than with differences in intelligence test scores. Training programmes are already being designed for people of different grades of intelligence, but perhaps one day training design will have to take into account *personality type* too!

To sum up, studies in the teaching of adults are helping to identify the factors which impede and facilitate performance in learning. There are good grounds for hope that as this field of knowledge grows we shall find new ways of overcoming difficulties and so make it possible to reach out to more people who currently give further education and training a nod of approval but a miss.

Further reading

BELBIN, E. and WATERS, P. Organised home study for older re-trainees in *Industrial training international* Vol. 2, No. 5, May 1967, pp. 196–98.

PYM, D., ed. *Industrial society: social sciences in management*. Penguin Books, 1969. Chap. 7, Belbin, E. and R. M. Retraining and the older worker.

ORGANISATION FOR ECONOMIC CO-OPERATION AND DEVELOPMENT *Training methods*; by R. M. Belbin. (Employment of older workers, 2) Paris: O.E.C.D., 1965; H.M.S.O.

ORGANISATION FOR ECONOMIC CO-OPERATION AND DEVELOPMENT *The discovery method: an international experiment in retraining*; by R. M. Belbin. (Employment of older workers, 6) Paris: O.E.C.D., 1969; H.M.S.O.

EMPLOYMENT AND PRODUCTIVITY, Dept. of *The discovery method in training*; by R. M. Belbin (Training information paper 5) H.M.S.O., 1969.

CLEUGH, M. F. *Educating older people* Tavistock, P., 1962.

JESSUP, F. W., ed. *Lifelong learning* Pergamon P., 1969.

EMPLOYMENT AND PRODUCTIVITY, Dept. of *The challenge of change to the adult trainee*; by D. B. Newsham. (Training information paper 3) H.M.S.O., 1969.

WELFORD, A. T. *Ageing and human skill* O.U.P., 1958.

LEARNING IN INDUSTRY
by A. O. Martin

Dr Martin is a Principal Psychologist at the Department of Employment and Productivity. In this chapter he describes how industrial retraining has changed under modern pressures, and suggests ways in which all teachers of adults, in or outside industry, can learn from industrial research and industrial experience in developing rapid and efficient teaching methods.

Introduction

The younger and the older

Why is it that a child of seven may be much more competent in using the telephone than a man of seventy? Simple questions like this are at the heart of all learning research which takes age into account. Older people gradually grew accustomed to the automatic telephone with letters and digits, but then they had to cope with STD and all-figure numbers. The child does not have to adapt from manual to automatic and then to STD; he goes straight to the new system. It is literally child's play to him. In the same way he will grow up with decimal coinage. Soon after that change we shall all have to think in terms of metres and litres instead of yards and pints. The pace of change accelerates for everybody, and it accelerates most rapidly in the world of work.

But *work* escapes definition. We may work much harder digging the garden at home than supervising an automatic process 'at work'; conversely, we may work much harder reading a technical report than reading a novel. Whatever we do demands some degree of mental or physical effort. The older we grow, the less inclined we become to involve ourselves in new forms of effort. We prefer the familiar, but the pace of change forces us to come to terms with the unfamiliar. Many jobs now performed in industry did not exist when the people doing them were at school, and the proportion will increase as new technologies become available. We may have to change our jobs three or four times in a life-time. We begin to realise that the real educational problem is *to learn how to learn* – to be more flexible and adaptable, yet also more discriminating. We can then anticipate change and determine its direction instead of merely being responsive to it.

A glance into history

In the Middle Ages, in the agricultural and handcraft days of our civilisation, learning and working went together. Formal education was largely vocational. The priesthood offered literacy and provided most of the leadership of the community. Thus to this day, the word 'clerical' has two distinct meanings. Training for crafts also developed and the Statute of Apprentices was passed in the days of the first Elizabeth. From this basis technical training evolved separately.

The Industrial Revolution created opportunities for mass leisure as well as wealth and we began to develop universal education 'for its own sake'. Technical training broadened through liberal studies and we are now witnessing the reintegration of the two mainstreams of *training* and *education* in a new way of looking at *learning*, the adaptive aspect of the single continuous process of living and working. Where have we got to at this point in time? What contribution is industry making to research into learning, and what contribution is learning research making to industry? Most of the research evidence on adult learning in fact comes from the world of work – people spend more time learning at work than learning during leisure.

The present system

Government training

The need for new skills was pointed up by two successive world wars. A good deal of learning research was carried out by the Government-sponsored Industrial Fatigue (later Health) Research Board during and after the first world war. Government then took a direct hand in the *accelerated vocational training* of adults and set up the first Government Training Centre (GTC) in 1925. Today there are 42 such centres in which some 15,000 people are trained or retrained each year. This part of the national system will expand until by early 1971 there will be 55 centres catering for some 22,000 people each year. The training is planned to keep pace with individual requirements and to meet the particular problems of adult learners.

After the second world war the Government training system was augmented by a new service of Training Within Industry (TWI) and by the establishment of an Instructor Training College (ITC). There are now two ITCs and five Instructional Training Units (ITUs) attached to GTCs, training about 3,000 people each year in the techniques of instruction. There are also 21 separately organised Industrial Rehabilitation Units (IRUs), mostly located adjacent to GTCs, which assess and condition the physically or mentally handicapped for a return to work. Many with the potential to learn new skills go on to GTC courses.

Training by industry

Adult learning to adapt to change cannot be rapid enough without the involvement of the leaders of industry and commerce. Who better than managers to take a direct hand in helping employees at all levels to make the best use of the new processes which managers introduce? The best firms have always recognised this. Many have Training and Education departments with a long history. Others lagged behind, and legislation was necessary.

The Industrial Training Act, 1964, empowers the First Secretary of State, Department of Employment and Productivity (DEP), to set up boards to oversee training in various sectors of industry. There are now 26 *industrial training boards* able to raise money by levies from the firms in their scope and to pay grants according to the quality and quantity of training carried out by each firm. Every board consists of representatives of employers, employees and educationists, all charged to ensure that the right training is being done in terms of quality and quantity, and firmly integrated with further education.

Central advice and information

The Central Training Council (CTC) advises the First Secretary and, indirectly, the industrial training boards. Its members are also representative of employers, employees and educationists. The main work is done by committees, one of which deals with research, and the job of the Research Committee is to advise the DEP on the need for new research, on the progress of existing projects and on how the results of research may be applied, particularly by training officers. The activities of the CTC Research Committee led to setting up a *training research information service*. This is run by the DEP to assist training officers and managers, the colleges responsible for training them, the CTC, the industrial training boards, research organisations, and the many voluntary organisations concerned with training.

The service is based on a linked system of publications:

1. a *Glossary of Training Terms*, which provides a means by which a common language of training may be developed;
2. a *Training Research Register*, published annually;
3. a *Training Abstracts Service* produced monthly for subscribers;
4. a series of *Training Information Papers* designed to report the results of research in a style likely to appeal to the lay reader.

Types of research

First, what do we mean by 'learning research in industry'? The word *research* can mean all things to all men. We speak of enquiries, surveys and investigations, which may be fact-finding exercises, reviews, case studies or theoretical discussions. We do laboratory and real-life experiments, which may be controlled or uncontrolled, and we do 'action research', which is specifically designed to improve the situation under observation. For the present purpose we will simply distinguish the lessons from direct practical experience from those of specific projects.

Direct experience

The direct experience of the Government training system, of the armed services, of individual firms, and of industrial training boards constitutes *learning research in industry* of a very practical kind. New methods of learning and teaching are tried out; ideally, the results are recorded and fed back into the national training system so that it can be improved. There is plenty of experience available in different sectors of the system – but much of it is still unused by other sectors and by the educational system. The systematic collection and dissemination of 'paper' information, through, for example, the DEP training research information service and the recommendations and newsletters sent out by industrial training boards, should itself help share experience more widely. But there is a limit to what people will read; we need more direct exchanges and visits, and wider use of the broadcasting media.

Specific projects

In the other category of research are carefully designed and monitored projects carried out mainly by independent organisations and financed, for example, by grants awarded by the DEP on the recommendation of the CTC Research Committee. There are about 30 recently completed and current projects of this kind. Two of them, being carried out on behalf of the BBC, relate to the effectiveness of broadcast industrial case studies in improving the knowledge and influencing the attitudes and decisions of managers. Projects are also sponsored by industrial training boards and other organisations. The *Training Research Register* lists over 250 projects.

Lessons from direct experience

The lessons from so many years of experience of industrial training would fill a substantial library. In this chapter we must be content with a few notes on some linked general trends:

1. the 'objective' approach;
2. the value of questioning;
3. managerial interest;
4. training specialists.

The 'objective' approach

The days are passing when 'courses' were designed at the desk by listing *topics* or *subjects* thought to be 'useful to the trainee'. We have become 'objective-minded' in two ways. First, we know we must identify training needs by analysing jobs very carefully and as objectively as possible. Second, such an analysis should result in *training objectives* stated in precise and measurable behavioural terms – that is, in terms of what people actually have to do. It should also result in training programmes in which the objectives of particular sessions are clearly related to the objectives of the programme as a whole.

In other words, the basic principles of programmed instruction – analysis, statement of objectives and their breakdown into steps – are increasingly applied to many forms of learning at work. The importance of programmed instruction is widely accepted. It is being practised by the DEP and by the industrial training boards, and a Programmed Instruction Centre for Industry has been set up at Sheffield to assist boards and firms. The 'objective' approach to learning at work pays handsome dividends. It pays dividends because it is *analytical*. It supplements creativity, insight and inspiration. It helps to tell us why new methods work effectively, and whether they can be applied elsewhere.

Objective analysis is also creative in its own right; it leads to new thinking. For example, training objectives are also *performance* objectives. The emphasis on job analysis thus encourages firms to introduce new or more realistic Experienced Worker Standards in an increasing range of jobs in industry and commerce. Similarly, managers at all levels are now more aware of the need to identify performance objectives for themselves and their staffs. This approach is now known as 'Management by Objectives'.

Finally, objective analysis has become essential nationally. The chief means by which industrial training boards seek to influence employers is the system of levy and grant. If a firm should receive a grant which fully reflects the quality and quantity of training carried out, then justice will not be possible until the effectiveness of training is measurable. Before the effectiveness of training can be assessed in terms of its financial costs and benefits (and more widely still, in terms of its full social costs and benefits), we have to be sure that training objectives are in fact being reached.

The value of questioning

A direct consequence of objective analysis is a sharper appreciation of the value of questioning, both as a learning/teaching method and as a technique of assessment. The analytical method *is* a questioning method. Likewise, all tests, examinations, subjective ratings and other methods used to assess the effectiveness of training are forms of questioning. The response of the learner to a question is not only a measure of the progress of learning; questioning is also one of the best possible means of ensuring that learning takes place. In this way we can see that assessment is not a separate activity but an integral part of the learning and training process. The more carefully the learning process is monitored, the more effective the learning is likely to be.

The fundamental importance of questioning cannot be over-emphasised. Being questioned by, and asking questions of, one's environment is the basis of all active learning – imitation, trial and error, discovery and insight. The 'environment' may be a human teacher, examination, book, film or anything else. Questions may be explicit or implicit, direct or indirect, oral or visual. However posed, they result in learning of some kind; efficiently posed, they result in efficient learning and in objective evidence that learning has taken place.

Managerial interest

Questions arouse interest. One of the lessons from direct experience is that the interest of supervisors and managers must be aroused if the learning of members of their staffs is to be improved. If the quality of learning is to be measured, managers and supervisors must set up adequate systems of training records, and link them with personnel records and performance records. It is quite impossible to develop cost/effectiveness measures without trying to separate out the influence of training from the influence of the many other factors which affect performance. Thus managers begin to ask themselves new questions. What kind of people am I selecting? How can I relate performance after training to the quality and quantity of production or service, to sickness and accident rates and other criteria by which I judge the general efficiency of my firm? When the need for training records is recognised, managers are thus stimulated to improve the 'information control' systems they already use.

They then begin to question the adequacy of their own 'learning to adapt to change'. They realise that they need help. Who can help managers and supervisors to learn more effectively? Certainly the future training of managers and supervisors must include *training* itself (a point which is now being recognised in the syllabus for the Diploma in Management studies) but they will not have time to specialise. They need training specialists to help the learning of everybody in the firm, at all levels. The emphasis is more and more on assisting *self-development* to complement formal training courses.

Training specialists

The role of the *instructor* in industry has long been recognised. The Government-sponsored Instructor Training Colleges and the

Training Within Industry Service have already been mentioned. Traditionally, from the earliest days of apprenticeship, learning was achieved by 'sitting by Nellie'. Nellie – or her male equivalent – is a powerful 'learning aid' if she knows the job thoroughly and if she has been thoroughly trained in the principles and techniques of instruction. And when we appreciate that the principles and techniques of instruction are very close indeed to the principles and techniques of good communication, we realise that all supervisors need this kind of training.

It is only in recent years that the *training officer* has shared the limelight with the instructor. He will usually be a full-time training expert, trained in the identification of training needs by appropriate methods of analysis, the construction and monitoring of training programmes, and the assessment of the effectiveness of training, as well as in the principles and techniques of instruction. There are currently about 33 universities and colleges running introductory courses for training officers, and the output during the 1967–1968 session was nearly 1,300 people. The courses are designed on a sandwich basis, with a minimum of four weeks in college and a project period in the firm.

The *project*, which is supervised by college staff who go to considerable lengths to stimulate the interest and involvement of managers, has proved to be a very rewarding aspect of the training programme. College tutors have been quick to see the implications for the design of the college-based aspects of the training. Their courses are increasingly active, participatory and practical, although in the early days many of them followed the more or less standard routine of 'lecture followed by discussion'. For example, training officers are not 'taught' chairmanship or report-writing – they practice these skills under guidance.

Lessons from specific research projects

The increasingly practical training of training officers results in an increasing use of participatory methods of training in industry – questioning, discussion, case studies, seminars and projects. The approach is no longer *teaching* – but *assisting learning*. We no longer speak of *training* aids – but of *learning* aids. This points immediately to the need to remove barriers to positive and efficient learning.

Questions arouse interest, but they can also arouse anxiety – perhaps the greatest barrier. It is with the removal of anxiety barriers that we shall be concerned in looking at some of the lessons to be drawn from specific research in the field of learning at work. The projects summarised below are reported in the DEP series of Training Information Papers.

'*The design of instruction*'

A number of projects with adult learners were undertaken to investigate the effectiveness of different ways of expressing the same written instructions. In general, simple declarative sentences were easier to understand than more complex grammatical forms. There is strong evidence to suggest that people grasp and use positive information more efficiently than the same information expressed negatively. The word 'not' as well as the less explicit negatives such as 'except', 'unless' and 'otherwise' should be avoided when possible. Negatives and exceptions arouse anxiety because they cloud the issue. The equivalent positive form of instruction may result in longer sentences, and even a certain amount of redundancy. However, verbal economy appears relatively unimportant compared with achieving the objectives of unambiguous and explicit instruction.

Here is an example of a difficult instruction:

'With the input selector control set at "switched", the timer can be started by connecting the green terminals or breaking a connection between the red, and stopped by reversing these operations.'

This is a long sentence of 36 words. We can replace it by three shorter sentences totalling 40 words – longer but much easier to understand and act upon:

'Set the input selector at "switched". Then start the timer by connecting the green terminals and stop it by breaking this connection. Alternatively, start it by breaking the connection between the red terminals and stop it by connecting them again.'

(Ideally, the timer should be designed to obviate alternatives!)

Another project also investigated the use of continuous prose to express complex interrelated rules, such as those contained in instruction manuals, regulations and legal agreements. The 'logical tree' method proved superior to continuous prose. A logical tree expresses rules either in the form of simple statements, ordering the rules from the most general to the most specific, or in the form of a visual graph or 'tree' which demonstrates the structure of the rules.

Both of these sets of projects illustrate the use of the principles of analysis and programming to reduce anxiety and to eliminate barriers to understanding.

These projects were concerned mainly with *written* instruction. But we can generalise with some confidence to *oral* instruction, particularly if we can supplement oral presentation with visual aids. We may generalise further by thinking about the very close connection between giving instruction in the sense of teaching and giving *instructions* in the sense of orders to be obeyed. Both are aspects of good communication, which facilitates learning, and the hallmark of good communication is that it is designed to meet the needs of the learner rather than those of the teacher or supervisor.

'*Identifying supervisory training needs*'

This work was also concerned with the facilitation of learning. The traditional way of training supervisors by running off-the-job courses based on 'what managers think their supervisors ought to know', has been superseded by the analytical approach – identifying training needs. The analysis of supervisors' jobs shows very clearly that all jobs are different. This means that there is a limit to the effectiveness of 'common courses'. The work suggests that an alternative or supplementary procedure is 'training by exception'. This goes straight to the problems encountered by each supervisor, that is to those issues which are exceptions to his normally adequate performance. It is the exceptions which arouse both interest and anxiety.

'Training by exception' puts the emphasis on the *individual*, but individual training is time-consuming. The old subject-package approach to *group* training is far easier to administer and a balance must be found. The problem in industrial training is the same problem in colleges and in all other institutions where adults learn. The task of the teacher, trainer or instructor is to assist the individual as a member of a group.

'*The challenge of change to the adult trainee*'

When one speaks of training by exception at supervisory level one is also speaking of the challenge of change. We – teachers, trainers and instructors – accept that we have to assist those for whose learning we are in part responsible. We ourselves also have to meet the challenge of change. This is a point which bears constant repetition. We all have to learn to accept adaptation as something that is continuous throughout life. We must adapt to change in our present jobs or adjust to the change which a new job demands.

Research has thrown light on the relationship between learning methods and the willingness of adult learners to remain in their firms. It showed that the learning methods of older workers were more significant than those of younger workers as far as retention in employment was concerned. Although a higher proportion of older men tended to leave during the training period or soon afterwards, their subsequent history was different. In the long term their 'survival rate' was better than the survival rate of the younger men.

The research was carried out in organisations known to be retraining workers over 35 years of age, as well as young workers, for operations which required a training period of at least two weeks. Older men tended to be most likely to succeed (as measured by turnover/retention figures) in those jobs requiring training periods of 10–13 weeks. They tended to 'survive' less well in those jobs requiring longer training periods or very short training periods and least well in those requiring 6–8 weeks.

Comparisons were made between groups trained by traditional on-the-job 'exposure' methods, those trained by 'systematic' methods based on analytical thinking, and those trained by special methods where the particular learning problems of older people had been considered. The systematic method proved no better *in relation to manpower turnover* than exposure training. However, it would be reasonable to suppose that jobs associated with high turnover would have been singled out for more detailed analysis and the application of modern principles of training. Thus the fact that systematic methods were used may merely reflect the existence of problem jobs. More research is required – to find out whether the job as such or the method of training was the more important variable in the situation.

The crucial finding of the research concerns the 'special method'. If the training procedure includes measures *designed to eliminate the difficulties of older learners* it tends to be followed by a markedly higher long-term survival rate for this group. The Industrial Training Research Unit, responsible for this research, has evolved concrete suggestions on how training can be suitably adapted for the older learner. It is appropriate to end this chapter by presenting these suggestions in summary form. The summary shows that learning research in industry has provided many practical lessons which others involved in teaching adults may usefully study. In the last chapter Dr Belbin (Consultant to the Unit) relates practical lessons to theory, and Mr Simpson refers to some of them in chapter 4.

Problems of learning for the adult

Suggestions for adapting training programmes to suit older learners.

1. *When tasks involve the need for short-term memory.*
   (a) Avoid the need for conscious memorising. This may often be accomplished by making use of 'cues' which guide the trainee.
   (b) When possible use a method which involves learning a task as a whole. If it has to be learned in parts, these parts should be learned in cumulative stages.
   (c) Ensure consolidation of learning before passing on to the next task or to the next part of the same task. (Importance of self-testing and checking.)

2. *When there is 'interference' from other activities or from other learning.*
   (a) Restrict the range of activities covered in the course.
   (b) Employ longer learning sessions than is customary for younger trainees.
   (c) Vary method of learning rather than the content of the course.

3. *When there is need to translate information from one medium to another.*
   (a) Avoid the use of visual aids which necessitate a change of logic or a change in the plan of presentation.
   (b) If simulators or training devices are to be used, they must be designed to enable learning to be directly related to practice.

4. *When there is need to 'unlearn' something for which the older learner has a predilection.*
   (a) Ensure 'correct' learning in the first place.
   (b) Employ an automatic feed-back system to convince the older learner of his errors.

5. *When tasks are 'paced'.*
   (a) Allow the older learner to proceed at his own pace.
   (b) Allow him to plan his programme within certain defined limits.
   (c) Aim at his beating his own targets rather than those of others.

6. *As tasks become more complex.*

   (a) Allow for learning by easy stages of increasing complexity.

7. *When the trainee lacks confidence.*

   (a) Use written instructions.

   (b) Avoid the use of production material too soon in the course.

   (c) Provide longer induction periods. Introduce the trainee very gradually both to new machinery and to new jobs.

   (d) Stagger the intake of trainees.

   (e) Avoid formal tests.

   (f) Don't give formal time limits for the completion of the course.

8. *When learning becomes mentally passive.*

   (a) Use an open situation which admits discovery learning.

   (b) Employ meaningful material and tasks which are sufficiently challenging to an adult.

Further reading

EMPLOYMENT AND PRODUCTIVITY, Dept. of *Glossary of training terms* H.M.S.O., 1967.

EMPLOYMENT AND PRODUCTIVITY, Dept. of *Training research register, 1968* H.M.S.O. 1968.

EMPLOYMENT AND PRODUCTIVITY, Dept. of *Training abstracts service: notes for users* The Dept., 168 Regent Street, London, W.1.

CENTRAL TRAINING COUNCIL *Third report to the Secretary of State* H.M.S.O., 1969.

EMPLOYMENT AND PRODUCTIVITY, Dept. of *The training and use of operators as instructors: a departmental report* H.M.S.O., 1969.

CENTRAL TRAINING COUNCIL *Training of training officers: introductory courses* H.M.S.O., 1966.

EMPLOYMENT AND PRODUCTIVITY, Dept. of *Design of instruction*; by S. Jones (Training information paper, 1) H.M.S.O., 1968.

EMPLOYMENT AND PRODUCTIVITY, Dept. of *Identifying supervisory training needs*; by P. B. Warr and M. W. Bird (Training information paper, 2) H.M.S.O., 1968.

EMPLOYMENT AND PRODUCTIVITY, Dept. of *The challenge of change to the adult trainee*; by D. B. Newsham (Training information paper, 3) H.M.S.O., 1969.

BARBER, J. W., ed. *Industrial training handbook* Iliffe, 1968.

SEYMOUR, W. D. *Industrial skills* Pitman, 1966.

MARTIN, A. Research in training in *Industrial training international* Vol. 3, no. 12, Dec. 1968, pp. 555–8.

LEARNING IN THE VOLUNTARY CLASS

by J. A. Simpson

In this chapter H. M. I. Simpson develops Dr Belbin's thesis on how adults learn by examining how it and the work of other research workers can be applied to students in voluntary adult education. He has some advice on the conduct of the first class, and on how to encourage the friendly, relaxed atmosphere which enables a group to work well. Mr Simpson is Staff Inspector with the Department of Education and Science.

You will have noted already that a great deal of educational thought, enquiry and research has been devoted to the job that we do as teachers, and to the best ways of doing it. There is no need to be daunted by the learned and complex nature of these studies, for it is, primarily, with their implications for work in the classroom that we are concerned, and there, they have to be adjusted to a particular set of circumstances which only the teacher knows first hand.

Teaching adults has obvious differences from teaching children in school. You don't get the kind of trouble that can arise among pupils who are compelled to attend, but, on the other hand, you've got students who, because they've come of their own free will, are equally free to stop coming. Instead of pupils in a class where all have much the same range of age and ability, you have adult students aged anything from twenty to seventy. In a woodwork class in a northern city I found that the oldest student was a retired Director of Education while the youngest was a girl of nineteen who worked in a soap factory. Your adult class will usually be very small as compared with a class in a school, but with a group of fifteen, or fewer, there arises the need for a much more personal relationship with each student, and all the possibilities of misunderstanding and friction are more serious. This is usually the first thing which strikes a schoolteacher taking an adult class for the first time – she is now dealing with individual people, fellow adults with all their differences of background and personality, some shy, some assertive, or demanding, some highly educated, some with a great deal of knowledge of the subject, some with none at all. Of course, the very smallness of the group makes it possible to give each a large amount of individual attention – and this is almost always a prime necessity.

Professor Jones has written about the different motives that bring people to our classes, and in any one class there are likely to be several different attitudes to it and to the subject. Some students may have come mainly for the sociability of the occasion, or because going to the institute, or centre, or university or WEA class, is a habit with them – part of their lives. Others are much more interested in the work itself – perhaps in mastering the subject as a whole, perhaps in preparing for a special occasion or producing a particular article. One lady left a class after the third meeting because she said she didn't just want to make a dress but to learn the craft of dressmaking. Teaching adults is a question of trying to please everybody in such a way that they all make the progress for which they are fit and willing – and a bit more. Again, the subjects which adults come to learn differ very much one from another – think of Yoga, Economics, Folk Dancing, Metalwork and Local History – and few suggestions about approach and methods can apply with equal force to them all. In the following notes I have thought mainly of the class in which people are learning practical or linguistic skills, rather than of subjects which are studied almost entirely by reading, lectures and discussion, and which are very often taught by people who have considerable expertise in this kind of teaching.

As I have already said, we know from research into adult education that a large number of our students come to us not only to learn something but to be with other people. Sometimes they come with a friend, but, in any case, they seek the satisfaction of sharing an experience and talking about it with others. The opportunities for this kind of contact and relationship which our courses offer are educative in themselves, and, as teachers, we can do a lot to make them more so. Far too many people today have no experience of group-life outside their family, where, we all know, it tends to be either routine or emotionally tense. Our class can soon become a group, if we give the right sort of encouragement, or it can remain a class composed of individuals and cliques. But quite apart from what the psychologists tell us about group-life, expert observers and our own experience both tell us that people work best when they are in a mentally comfortable atmosphere – not strained by doubts and curiosity about their neighbours. The teacher's part in all this amounts to little more than that of a thoughtful host or hostess, seeing that people get to know each other, understand each other, getting them to talk, bringing them into the picture. Of course, a first step is for the teacher to get to know the students and something of each of them. We know ourselves what a difference it makes to be addressed by our name (Americans would say by our Christian name). Teachers of adults can never make too much use of people's names, and it is not difficult in teaching or discussion to bring in some additional information. 'You were saying last time, Mrs. Smith, that you had found a way of getting over this difficulty.' A good deal in effective teaching is made up of such apparent trivialities. Nevertheless, they may involve some preparatory thinking, and, if our memory for detail is not excellent, the jotting of some notes at the right time.

It is easy to see how important is the first class-meeting of a course, and how much the future of it will depend upon the atmosphere created then. Incidentally, the business of 'calling' a register can introduce a starchy note, and it can be avoided by appointing a class secretary who will compile the register and, thereafter, fill it in unobtrusively. This procedure makes for relationship among the students. Still, whatever else brings the students to us, they expect to learn about the subject and in this respect, also, the first meeting is of great importance. It has been noted by those who study these things that the older students become, the more they like a clear picture in advance of what they are going to do and be asked to do, and of where the course is going to take them. There is no need, as perhaps with children, to win them over gradually and imperceptibly into an interest in the subject so that they work without noticing it and are surprised, later, at what they've learned. Adults are not put off by hearing about the tasks ahead; indeed, they like it, and it is useful to be able to tell them what stages of knowledge and skill the whole course will cover. For this reason the teacher should have a fairly detailed plan of the course – a syllabus – not merely the brief description that is printed in the brochure or other publicity. It is very useful to spend plenty of time at the first meeting discussing this syllabus and amending it – adapting it to the wishes of individual students to learn particular things or have help with a project of their own. It is of vital importance that the views of all students shall be heard at this early stage. Terrible tales are told of students who sat through the first two meetings of their class without the teachers' having, it seems, noticed their presence. And for many students in craft or dress classes it is a frustrating experience merely to be asked, 'What do you want to make?' – as if the teacher had nothing to teach. So a statement of what is to be taught, a detailed syllabus, serves many purposes.

The same consideration of adult characteristics should hold good for all the subsequent meetings of the class. It has been found that adult students want to get on with a clearly defined job and to work steadily towards its conclusion. There is not in their case any need for contrived breaks or changes of method – the sort of thing which for children is provided by 'playtime' or a learning-game or a film. The adult is usually quite happy to settle into a sustained session of work for which he or she has received clear instructions or guidance. He works best at his own individual rate. This means that teaching to the whole group should never exceed what is necessary for a progressive course, leaving plenty of time for individual tuition in which the teacher hears or watches the student at work, notices faults and difficulties, and helps the student to acquire higher standards of performance and greater ability to judge and choose, to create and design for himself. Again, unless one has a splendid memory, it is useful to make a note of the individual stage of progress of each student so that the teacher can, next time, ensure that the student's work moves him on from there.

Dr Belbin has reminded us of how much more readily people learn by discovering things for themselves than by following written instructions or reading books or listening to oral teaching. We should do all we can in our teaching to make the most of this fact. It would, however, be unwise to try to make learning by discovery the sole method of work, under the circumstances which prevail in most of our non-vocational classes. In the schools, this heuristic method, as it is called, is very highly regarded, but, even there, where the resources are far greater than in adult classes, its application has to be restricted by the heavy demands it makes on the time of the teachers and pupils and by risks it may involve of damage to the children or equipment. In adult classes these restrictions have greater force, for, usually, teacher and students have only one lesson each week, and with limited access to premises and equipment. It falls to the teacher to ensure that the students have a secure framework in which to learn, and a sense of continuity and progression. It is her responsibility, too, to see that the lesson-time is employed as usefully as possible for all the students, who have to pay a substantial proportion of the costs in fees. Moreover, they do not wish to waste or spoil the materials which they must purchase, but look forward to an end-product for use in real life. Thus, their situation differs from that of children in the schools or industrial trainees engaged upon mock exercises with provided materials. But, apart from the question of time and materials, we have to remember that in non-vocational classes the desire to learn is only one – and not necessarily the strongest – of the motives that bring students to us. Quite commonly they have only a confused idea of the subject and would be bewildered and disheartened if left too much to themselves. The principle of learning by discovery is a valid one, but for such students it should be applied within a firm framework of exposition and instruction to the class as a whole, and of helpful individual tuition which prevents frustration or irretrievable mistakes. Adults are very quick to feel that they are 'getting nowhere', – that they are being under-challenged. Sometimes a teacher will notice that several students have a similar difficulty and will take this opportunity of giving tuition to the class as a whole. Expert observers have noted that adults, in learning, are much less stimulated by competition and comparison with others than is the case with children. In fact, the example of a neighbour's progress can have a negative effect upon adults, and it is much more useful for a teacher to direct the attention of students to how their work at present compares with what it was, say, a month ago, than to point to the achievements of the star performer of the class.

Dealing with people individually in our teaching, and having such a broad age-range in our class, it can be very helpful for us to bear in mind some of the things that the experts – doctors, psychologists, educationists – have noted about the different stages of adult life. Contrary to some rather simple legal thinking which divides mankind into the young and the grown-up, as if all life after eighteen or twenty-one were a changeless, undeveloping thing, there are, as we all know, a number of quite clearly marked biological stages in adult life – although these stages occur at different ages in different people – and adjustment to each brings its own problem and characteristics which affect people's will and capacity to learn. According to the anthropologists there are, also, a number of identifiably different human types, each with its own characteristics of physique and temperament, so that, as Dr Belbin has suggested, we have to become

49

accustomed to very varied attitudes to learning and responses to our teaching. Do people lose the power to learn, including the learning of things which involve bodily movements, as they grow older? The experts tell us that, if we leave aside the effects of diseases like rheumatism, there is some loss of this ability as the years roll on, but that it is very small, and negligible in relation to other things which make people slow or quick to learn. These other things include the sort of intelligence and physical structure with which we were born, and, also, the extent to which we have kept on, since we left school, practising the skills of learning – whether in using tools and implements, or making music or memorising a vocabulary and imitating a tone of voice. So that, for the most part, differences among people as to their habit of learning and their general intelligence and physique are much more important in helping a teacher to estimate what to expect from a student than any difference in age. All this underlines the need to think in terms of the progress being made by individual students, rather than having some standard for the class as a whole. If these considerations sound formidably complicated, it may reassure you to know that in more than twenty years of visiting classes I have almost never encountered a student who was gaining no benefit at all from the teaching.

There is, however, some evidence that the older adult student – say, those over thirty-five or forty – tends to forget what he has learned more readily than younger people. This means the need in classwork for much more practice at a process until it is mastered and, also, frequent return to it. As adults are less patient of reminders, this revision has to be introduced tactfully and not put across as sheer revision but put in some new setting so that it has a progressive appearance. Moreover, the older adult student, from what research workers into adult learning tell us, finds it much harder to recognise his own errors, to see and understand just where he is going wrong – for example in making a series of manual movements or pronouncing a phrase. Indeed, he or she, finds it hard, often, to accept the fact that there is any error at all unless there is immediate proof. This is why teaching machines that 'ring up' error at once are particularly useful with adult classes, but they are not applicable to the majority of practical subjects. So it is one of the foremost parts of the job of the teacher of these subjects to watch the individual student's work carefully, diagnose the faults as they occur, and explain them to the student, breaking them down into each stage of the sequence of movement so that the precise moment of error can be seen. A similar process is a most important part of the tutorial work of tutors in lecture and discussion subjects. Sometimes students show a general bewilderment and slowness, with frequent hold-up, and it is necessary then to talk generally with them, trying to get them to think out precisely what are the difficulties they find, what is the core of their problem.

Although earlier on I mentioned films to say that their use as mere relief had little merit in teaching adults, there can be no doubt that the use of visual aids – films, film-strips, slides, charts, or even the humble chalk-board – is of tremendous importance in this work. One of the firmly established features of growing older is that as people age they tend to depend increasingly upon sight rather than hearing for receiving information; and that information received visually makes a more lasting impression upon them. Unfortunately it is also true that quite early in life our powers of vision begin to decline and in the case of many middle-aged people this decline is quite serious. Thus a great responsibility rests on the teacher to ensure that students are really seeing demonstrations, or even their own work, adequately – not always an easy business in rooms which are fitted with lighting designed for only occasional use in the day-time for keen-eyed youngsters. Teachers do right to press for the installation of suitable lighting for adult purposes. But, apart from this, visual aids like films and slides can do a great deal which it is simply not possible to do by 'live' demonstration. They can break a process up into its component parts, or show it in slow-motion. 'Stills' and diagrams and charts and pictures and models can be available for constant re-examination by the student. Experienced teachers usually have not only a stock of these aids for immediate use, but also lists of material of this kind which could be useful in their subject, and they keep their eyes open for additions to it. It is not only educational firms that produce it but also many commercial concerns and public utility corporations like the Gas Council. Once again, I can only say that if there is not sufficient equipment or space for the use or display of visual aids, then it is up to the teacher to demand it. This may require a certain persistence, but adult education is still at the stage where this kind of pressure for suitable conditions has to be listed among the techniques of good teaching. The teacher who has insisted that the room is properly equipped and arranged in a seemly fashion so that the students have no cause for feeling that they are temporary intruders amidst a hostile bristle of stacked chairs – that teacher has done much.

Because they depend so much on what they see, older people can often learn better from the printed than the spoken word. Against this, however, one must set the fact that attitudes to, and, indeed, ability at, reading vary a great deal from person to person. Still it is likely that a certain amount of the content of any lesson can best be conveyed in duplicated, typewritten notes. Of course, the students should be encouraged to make their own notes, – and many teachers state at the outset of the course that a notebook is essential, and sell one there and then to the students. But we cannot hide from the fact that many students, and not always the least progressive, will do little in the way of note-making. The same sort of common sense should be applied to books in our work. There will be some students in most practical classes for whom a substantial book would be a confusing, if not depressing, proposition. By contrast, most classes contain students who can and do get a great deal out of suggestions by the teacher of books on the subject which convey a deeper knowledge of processes or which widen the subject by showing something of the sciences that underlie it or of its social and historical background. A sensible practice that is often adopted is for the teacher to have a small collection of books for display and borrowing in the classroom, including some simple and well-illustrated volumes; and, also, to distribute a reading list of other books, and chapters in books, recommended for study, consultation or general interest.

One thing that is easily forgotten by the teacher of adults is that there is a pool of knowledge and expertise waiting to be tapped among the students themselves. When we teach we are all prone to think that we must ourselves be the source of all information. It is much less of a strain on us, and much more useful to the student, if we take the line that anyone in the group may be able to contribute a particular piece of expertise or knowledge better than we can. An experienced observer of our work wrote about the dressmaking classes at one big institute:

'Some of the students had considerable skill in using a sewing machine and were accustomed to industrial making-up processes. It seemed a pity that these skills were unnoticed by the instructors either as a basis of class discussion, or a basis for the use of good industrial methods in teaching.'

This reference to discussion is, of course, of tremendous importance. One of the most common ways in which classes in practical subjects fall short of their educative possibilities is in the lack of any discussion. This is not the place to go into all the conclusions of research departments about group dynamics and the group process. Its application to the adult class has been much studied here and in America, and Mr Brown touches on it later in this book. It is enough here to note that it all points to the conclusion that students are influenced much more by the expression of their own and others' opinions as it emerges in discussion than by anything which is urged on them by a teacher standing, as it were, over against them. There is no reason why the teacher must maintain this detached position, particularly with fellow adults. Rather, he or she can be a specially skilled member of the group, participating, man to man, in a non-authoritative way, in information discussion. In this kind of exchange people are led to put into words ideas towards which they have been fumbling and which, often to their surprise, they realise they have made their own. It is in discussion as between equals that some of the most important things in education get done. And, at a more obvious level, discussion is one of the chief ways in which the wider educational possibilities of a subject can be brought into the classwork, and Mr George Whittle stresses the desirability of this, and makes practical suggestions about it, in another chapter of this book. Very many of our classes are composed of small groups, with students working all at conversational distance from each other, and often engaged on manipulative tasks during which they can hear and participate in discussion according to individual inclination. Disappointingly little use is made of this situation. This is probably because many teachers fear that discussion may get into realms where they are no longer the expert with all the answers. Not long ago I was present during the following conversation – all of it quite audible to every member of the class:

First Student (to her neighbour) Do you think that's about an inch?
Second Student Yes – about that. I wish I could do *this*.
First Student It looks all right to me. You've got checks. I wish I had.
Second Student Well – it's terribly hard to put together.
First Student Oh, I put mine together whether they match or not.
Teacher (coming across) When you set in sleeves you've got to watch that. That tacking has to be very sharp. You want them to look smart.

First Student Well, I often wonder what 'smart' is. I suppose it's something to do with expensive – or what?
Teacher (After short pause) Well – nice (breaks off conversation).

When, later, I asked the teacher – a first-rate craftswoman with industrial experience – why she didn't make this a talking point for the whole class, she said, very understandably, that it was a difficult subject on which she couldn't give the answer. But, as we all know, on this kind of question which touches on what it is that makes human beings tick, and what kind of society we make for ourselves, no one, teacher or student, can have 'the right answer', but everybody has some opinion worth hearing, everyone has something to learn. This, of course, brings us back to what Dr Belbin has so wisely said about learning by discovery, and to his statement that 'it is through the contribution of class members that discoveries are made'.

Most aspects of life today are changing rapidly, and new inventions and techniques are coming each year into use in education, based on new discoveries about how people behave and learn. That is one among many reasons why it would be foolish to take anybody's advice, including mine, about teaching, as the last word. In any case, in human relationships there is no royal road and every teacher must weigh advice against his own experience and own circumstances. As far as new inventions and teaching techniques are concerned, it is, perhaps, rather comforting to learn from the educationists that adults usually react less favourably to them than do younger people, and that adults tend to like best those methods of learning which they have used in the past.

Perhaps some of the suggestions I have made may seem to you as if they would reduce the appeal of your class, and would make your teaching off-putting for some of your students. I know how important this is but, after serious thought, I can only say that I don't think it would be the case. I have some confirmation from a survey, taken in one large establishment, of the reasons for 'drop-out' or wastage from classes. The chief reasons which students gave for giving up going to their class were, in this order:

1. The standard of work was too low.
2. Not enough work was set for them between classes.
3. The subject was presented uninterestingly.
4. There was not enough discussion.

Further reading

HARRIES, G. M. and SUTHERLAND, C. *Education through crafts* Llandaff, Cardiff: Training College of Domestic Arts for S. Wales and Monmouthshire, 1960.

ROBERTSON, S. *Creative crafts in education* Routledge, 1952.

ROBERTSON, S. M. *Craft and contemporary culture* Harrap, 1961.

NORTHERN ADVISORY COUNCIL FOR FURTHER EDUCATION *Suggestions for part-time teachers of women's subjects* Newcastle: The Council, 4th edn. 1963.

YORKSHIRE COUNCIL FOR FURTHER EDUCATION *Handbook for part-time teachers* Leeds: The Council, 2nd edn. 1950.

STYLER, W. E. *Questions and discussion* Workers' Educational Association, 1952.

THE ROLE OF THE TEACHER
by Richard Hoggart

This chapter is about some of the dangers and temptations that beset the adult education teacher and how to avoid them – intellectual flabbiness, smugness, showing off, or sometimes plain dullness – a formidable list. In the last part of the chapter Professor Hoggart discusses how best to evaluate students' work.

Richard Hoggart is Director of the Centre for Contemporary Cultural Studies at the University of Birmingham.

I believe, from thinking about my own temptations, that the main occupational risk for an adult education teacher is intellectual flabbiness. You are not sufficiently often challenged. Your colleagues are likely to be scattered far and wide, or on different shifts. You don't meet them in regular seminars or simply over coffee from day to day, or argue with them at staff meetings about the point of the examination questions you propose setting or the shape of a syllabus or a reading-list. Most public examinations are hard to defend and liberal adult education is the better for being without them. But one thing they may provide for the tutor himself: a simple, practical check on the coherence, level and progress of his teaching.

The situation is made trickier because students in adult education tend to be deferential. They look up to the tutor too readily and this tempts some of us into over-easy relationships, relationships not taut enough for good teaching. In adult education conferences, one can often recognise tutors of long standing. They look nice but a bit unchallenged, a bit too relaxed in their friendliness. They tend to suck pipes ruminatively, to wear shapeless pepper-and-salt tweeds, to have pleasant crinkly smiles. They are not aggressive or over-strained, they don't puff nervously on cigarettes, they don't look as though they have been trained in public relations. They look very decent and helpful. You can visualise them sitting on the edge of the table in front of an adult class, swinging their legs, genuinely friendly, not at all pushing, saying: 'It all depends what you mean by . . .' or 'That's a very good point, Mrs Johnson, but I wonder whether you've considered . . .'. Even more than most teaching, adult education invites its tutors to a range of attractive self-deceptions, forms of role-playing. The worst forms are the nicest because they encourage attitudes towards the students and their abilities which, though well-intentioned, are forms of patronage. They don't lead you to test the students or yourself to the top of their or your bent. The price you pay, over the years, for this too-easily adopted role of kindly sage, this endless fence-sitting, is intellectual slackness.

Inevitably, there are many variants. The most obvious is the man who is over-fond of his own voice, who too obviously 'likes to hear himself speak'. A smile appears on his face as he talks, as though he is actually tasting the sound of his own rolling periods; or you can recognise the element in yourself by the feeling of almost physical pleasure when you are led into that kind of rhetoric. It's like finding you can fly, for a few yards. Those of us who were brought up in the Nonconformist chapel tradition are especially at risk here – the combination of rhetoric, earnestness and the urge towards charismatic relationships is heady. Welshmen – chapel, plus song, plus rich deep voices – are the worst risks of all. The Danes, with their Grundtvigian background – the Folk, the Land and the Word – are high risks too. Welshmen in Danish adult education summer schools are formidably rhetorical personalities.

The urge towards a generalised charismatic relationship, that way of showing-off one's personality which ends in the rhetoric of a lay preacher, is the strongest of all temptations. You have to learn to suspect those evenings when you feel a throb come into your voice, your eye seems bright and eager, and the students look up at you with a touch of wondering admiration. Two types of teacher – in any kind of education, but adult education is an especially dangerous area in these ways – should particularly be suspected: the charismatic, an imaginative pied piper of Hamelin; and the systems-builder, an intellectual pied piper of Hamelin, who offers a complete guide and system to experience. Men who are a combination of both – some types of Marxist are like that – are the most dubious. Any teacher who begins to acquire fans, disciples, followers, ought to suspect himself until he has examined as honestly as he can the nature of these relationships. He may well be getting between the students and their own hold on the subject. We should be glad to be judged by the degree to which our students stand on their own feet, out of our shadows. Which means we have to try to make sure they retain their freedom to be critical of us. Or, if that sounds too grand, ironic about us and towards us.

Because we are so little tested from outside, by day-to-day contact with colleagues, we have to try to frame our lives so that we are faced with challenges, not over-worryingly but steadily. The most obvious way to ensure this is to contribute to one's subject itself (to the subject, not simply to the teaching of the subject), so that we are in contact, even though at long distance or longish intervals, with very good minds in that subject. Or we may be able to attend regular staff seminars at the nearest university. Much more important is the challenge that can come from within the class itself, from really looking at and listening to the class members. Once we have taken the measure of the temptation to get swollen-headed in teaching adult education classes and begun really to look at and listen to our students, we discover that in any class there are several people who are in some ways actually or potentially better equipped than we are. Which comes back to the point above, about not getting between them and the experience. We have to do what we can to give them the chance to develop in their own best way – though we can know very little about what that best way may be for any one student, and our particular contribution to it will be and ought to be relatively minor.

Again, this comes back to making the atmosphere in the class consistently critically alert, rather than pally or admiring. We have to break the slightly smothering caul of respect for the tutor, so that students can criticise our work honestly and openly. I don't mean aggressively, though I would rather have some aggression than pussy-footing. It is hard enough for a student to be articulate in class-discussion without having one hand tied behind his back by the wrong kind of respect or friendliness towards the tutor. I was given a chance to learn this particular lesson early, since in my very first class-meeting, a young woman – experienced in the classes of a good older tutor – stood up when the 'discussion period' began and frankly criticised the way I had conducted the first hour. I had read a prepared lecture, out of nervousness.

We and they need to be involved, testing each other all the time, not working from stock materials or stock positions. Doing that without being in the last resort personally involved on either side, without having our sense of self-identity bound up with the class.

There are many ways in which that kind of unhealthy relationship can develop, for both students and tutors. We have to give the students room, so far as we are able to help here, to steer clear of the wrong relationships, so that they can find their own intellectual identities better. Then the kinds of class-and-tutor or individual-and-tutor relationships which *can* be healthy and useful may also emerge. They will only emerge from this more direct and honest base, not from being encouraged as ends in themselves, or vaguely regarded as the necessary foundations for good teaching and learning. Brought in too soon or too directly, they are false foundations.

It is as well to realise, first, how *little* one can do in any one class meeting or one session. This wonderfully sharpens the mind towards working-out what best one can do and how to do it. It also inhibits that sort of breast-feeding, that over-maternalism characteristic of enthusiastic but vague or nervous teachers. We all know about the pointlessness of cramming students with facts. We recognise less the dangers of smothering them with our own attitudes and responses. Some English teaching, for instance, is so backward that it does attempt to cram data into students. The more characteristic defect of English teaching is an unthinking or selfish attempt to transmit attitudes, prescribed opinions. There should be no received opinions or attitudes. Every book studied is a new book, being read for the first time. More in English than in other subjects the old saw applies: you are not giving something; you are trying to make something happen. What you can help to happen, in any one class-meeting of two hours, may seem little but can be important – a new way of looking, a new insight, a better grasp on ordering and so on – or the beginnings of such qualities; they may only be retained, and made part of the student's frame of mind, after several weeks or months.

If we work on these lines, we find that most of our regular students can take as much as we can give, so long as we avoid those devices, those ways of making the subject a mystique, which are really ways of hiding behind it, of refusing to come out into the open for fear of being challenged. If we bend our minds to them, most things can in the end be said fairly simply, at least the kind of things most of us are trying to say. Most things we have to say can be stripped down to understandable elements without loss. In adult teaching, most technical languages can be dispensed with; or, where they are necessary, they can be slowly built up and justified throughout a session. Virtually all knowing allusions or name-dropping of references can be relegated to the syllabus or the book-lists. There is never any justification for starting a sentence: 'As Chomsky says, of course . . .' or 'We recall, naturally, that Wittgenstein argued . . .'. We don't recall any such thing, neither the students nor us. *They* didn't know it before; and it didn't come to *us* lightly, from our well-stocked minds – we noticed it when we were working with our books at our desks. Once stripped down in this way, many of our points begin to seem obvious or tautologous – which is a gain. It is a gain for us as intellectuals and as teachers, and a gain for the students. It makes the odds in the classroom more even, between us and them; and it makes the odds between different kinds of students, graduate and non-graduate, more even too. This procedure taxes both us and the students. But if we do lose any students by it, they are as likely as not to be graduates who treasure their degrees and tend to feel superior to, say, a motor mechanic or a secondary-modern-school housewife in the class; and who find by this method, though their degree has given them the ability to move among received opinions, that out in the open where mind and feelings come freshly to a text, they have no special ability and may even find the work harder than those not shaped by study for a degree.

Obviously, to work like this requires careful preparation. Adult education teaching is not a soft option, fag-end work we can tuck in somehow, no matter how tired we may be. As much if not more than other forms of teaching, it demands energy if it is to be done well. It is a delicate balancing act, and if we are tired we will simply fall off. I am always surprised to discover that roughly the same sort of material with roughly the same sort of group can go either very well or very badly – according to my own grip on any particular evening, my own tiredness or freshness.

Throughout, I am thinking chiefly of the problems of teachers in the arts and humanities. Probably teachers of languages and crafts are less tempted to these kinds of attitudes and intellectual postures. Others, with more knowledge than I have, will say something elsewhere in this book about their special problems. From such experience as I have had, though, I would risk this generalisation: that if the main temptation of the humanities tutor is over-stylishness, that of the teacher of more straightforwardly content-bound subjects is an *inadequacy* of style. There is an over-tight sticking to 'the book', to what has to be 'got through'. Here, the main complaint among students is of just plain dullness; and it probably stems from both a lack of

confidence and a failure to realise – a failure not at all helped by the general climate – that the teaching of even the most 'routine' subjects need not be at all routine, is an exciting field for experiment, and at the moment a wide-open field. So what can we do ? Take risks. Take time off for a few half-hours each week to ask ourselves why we think our subject is interesting, no matter what the world outside says about it. (If we can't find convincing reasons perhaps that's a fair warning that we would be happier elsewhere.) Ask ourselves – it is intrinsically a very interesting question – how the subject hangs together in our own minds, what is the structure or pattern or shape of our grasp of it; and then ask ourselves where the students are at the moment, intellectually and imaginatively, in their relation to the subject's possibilities. Finally, how can they be brought to have at least the sort of grasp on the subject that we have ? At this point we are ready to take big risks; and there is not likely to be any more a feeling of dullness or repetition.

In planning each evening the object is to keep the class taut, varied and full. But not hectic either; which means that there will be varieties of pace and tone – and spaces between. I am not suggesting that all this can be deliberately planned in advance. But that, roughly, is how it is likely to come out, though much of it will be decided on the spot, taken as it comes, with *ad hoc* decisions being made all along the way. I suppose hardly anyone nowadays uses the old division of a class meeting into one-hour-talk and one-hour-discussion. Just how best the two hours should be broken up will vary with the subject or the needs of a particular aspect of a subject, or of a particular evening. Even if there is some quite sustained presentation by the tutor early in the evening, or at intervals throughout it, it won't normally be material read in consecutive sentences and paragraphs for a con-siderable length of time. But even this is not an absolute rule; almost any type of teaching can have a point with some subjects, some tutors, some students and some stages in learning. One can present an argument which seems important for that evening in several different ways and from several angles. One is trying to measure all the while the extent to which the point is being understood, how far the students are able to engage critically with it. As far as possible, one makes it concrete; or, alternatively, translates the concrete into the abstract so that the students have the chance to grasp a new – even if small – intellectual pattern or movement. And so on, in many varieties of approach and stress, staying with what seems a useful point until, so far as one can bring it about, each member of the class has seen the point, is in a position to begin to 'make it his own'. This steady going backwards-and-forwards with a group requires a good deal of honest-trading in relationships, and a low degree of embarrassment about speaking publicly by the class members. One is, to repeat a point made earlier since what I've just said has been filling it out, not so much giving as 'putting in the way of'.

None of this can be done properly without a thoroughly-planned syllabus, one thought out tactically and strategically. Neither the tutor nor the student should be in doubt about the overall aims of the course and its larger pattern of working over the session; nor about the place of each week in that pattern; nor about the shape of any one week in itself. The syllabus should be as clear a guide as we can make it, and so should its partner – the reading-list. A reading-list is not a bibliography, a more or less impressive list of whole books. It is a tool which will include whole books, probably grouped in several lists according to their importance to the particular course; it will just as valuably include parts of books, advice on specific chapters, on magazine articles, on cheap editions and so on.

It follows that part of each weekly session will need to be devoted to establishing where you are in the syllabus and where you hope to go next, to helping fill out the sense of a coherent journey. Similarly, each week, something will need to be said about the reading which is to follow, both short-term reading for the next meeting and long-term, background or preparatory reading for the next main phase of the course. If the course is to achieve anything like what it sets out to do, not only the tutor but also the students must prepare in advance, regularly and for both short and long-term goals. They must prepare, week by week, by reading and writing. It is a joint matter, but one in which the tutor has primary responsibility for keeping the lines taut.

There may not be a long, set 'discussion period' but there will be a lot of discussion, sometimes for substantial periods at a time. 'Socratic procedures', we usually say, and this is right. But we need to define more thoroughly what we mean by 'Socratic'. We shouldn't mean baiting or elaborate dangling or elegant fence-sitting. We should mean helping the students to think and feel for themselves by carefully-phrased questions – serious, relevant but not proselytising questions – designed to set them off in enquiry on their own and in their own ways. We should mean raising alternatives, making contrasts, so that they are stimulated into making the right jumps themselves. To work in this way is difficult, the hardest discipline of all for the tutor. It is so much easier just to *tell* them, or lead them straight to an open door. The right procedure is much more like, to borrow an image from I. A. Richards, providing hand-holds or pointing to cracks in the rocks, to which they must stretch and then hoist themselves over to the next level. The point is the muscular development, not the height reached.

For some of us, the greatest difficulty of all is to control *ourselves*, to listen without intervening. Knowing when to shut up has all sorts of aspects: it means knowing that it may be best to keep silent even though there is a pause, because that may allow a student who has been thinking quietly to contribute, perhaps in a way one wouldn't have suspected; it means resisting the temptation to short-circuit the whole procedure by giving too many little lubricating lecturettes – clever, perhaps, and even illuminating, but still not as useful as the students' finding their own way in their own time. It means, most of all, shutting up so as to listen better until we hear what is really being said behind often clumsily-chosen words. When we do that, it is surprising how often what is being said is intelligent and sensitive, more intelligent and sensitive than our training and assumptions might have led us to guess. We are, for the n'th time, trying to provide a ground on which they find things out for themselves. Though, of course, we also have to try to learn to recognise when it will be useful if we do intervene, when there is a prospect not of fruitful silence but of sagging emptiness. We have to try to learn which students will gain by being encouraged to contribute in discussion, and for which of them that direct invitation might be a setback and personally painful. It isn't always right to assume one can or should get all the silent ones to speak in the group.

We need to have a fair idea of possible lines for the discussion, of several main points which seem, in advance – given the subject at this point, and the state of a particular class – likely to be most useful to pursue. With alternatives, so far as one can see. But this is not a *programme* for discussion. It is available as one possibility. We have to be ready to scrap the whole or parts of it, to shift direction, divert for a while, according to the needs of the actual situation. Sometimes an unexpected difficulty will keep the class stuck near what we thought would be the first of several points, and one of the easiest. Sometimes someone, or the group as a whole, will throw up an approach better than any we had thought of in advance, and we must then follow that line. All of which means being as alert and responsive and open and unjealous as we can; and making decisions on the run.

So far I have said more about the group as a whole than about the individual students. When a good adult class is working well, it is a community of a special and unusual kind and very valuable for all its members, including the tutor. The activity of the group as a whole, in a good discussion session, pushes on for all, is an integral part of, the education offered. Still, the more important question in the end is what happens to the individual students, to each separate member of the class. To the tutor's understanding of what is being achieved by each member, and in what ways he can help any one person, the best single guide is the students' written work. This is why justifications for not asking for written work, or for only asking for it irregularly or in an undemanding way – justifications which are quite common nowadays – do not wash. They are anti-educational. Written work is immensely the best guide we have to the needs of each individual; nothing else, not even the most apparently rewarding group discussions or private talks, can take its place.

Written work has, so far as possible, to be tailored to the needs of each individual, to be seen as part of a larger relationship – of letters exchanged between class-meetings, short private discussions before or after class, individual guidance on reading. In this way, we are less likely to fail to know each student as a distinctive individual, with distinctive problems and possibilities. Since most adult classes are small, this doesn't seem too much to ask. It follows that the marking has to be particularly close and detailed. It may run from pedestrian matters of grammar to a quite elaborate taking-up of issues; but always it should aim to be practically and positively helpful. Good marking is time-consuming and demands close attention; a set of ticks in the margins, a few hieroglyphics and 'Thank you very much. Keep it up.' at the end are just not sufficient.

For what is the point of 'marking' in adult education? By what criteria does one assess the work? By its comparison with, say, internal university essays? Or by the distance of each particular individual from the point at which he started out, or reached in his last essay? These are not mutually exclusive; yet there can be no real doubt about the general direction an answer ought to take. It has two aspects. We, the teachers, should aim at as high a standard as our own minds are capable of reaching. It can't be higher or better, but shouldn't be worse. Because, again, properly guided most students will also be able to reach it. That standard will be established not by overt statements or mark-schemes, but in all sorts of implicit ways.

The second aspect is the establishing of standards for the students; and they will differ with each individual. Here, our objective is to help each one as far as we can to reach his or her own next best standard at each stage of the class. With these two elements in play – the tutor's objectives and the standards defined by those, and each student's possibilities and the standards defined by them – we can avoid the rigidity of fixed external standards which ignore the different needs of each student; and we can avoid that sloppy relativism which doesn't stretch *any* student because 'they are all, in their own ways, doing wonderfully'. We can avoid, too, competition between students because that is irrelevant and damaging.

The only people who are being judged from outside are us, the tutors; and that by the demands of the subject, which we have to respect. So we can't define standards for the students until we have defined for ourselves the objectives of our teaching, and the standards these therefore demand from us. The standards possible for each student will then take time to emerge. We have to build up, steadily but as soon as we can, a graph of each student's needs, possibilities, failings. This means not only writing a great deal on his essays – which is for our benefit as much as for his, since it clears our minds to write our reactions down – but keeping notes on each student. We may think we have good memories and can retain a clear sense of what each student was like at the start, where his essays began to pick up and in what way, what main weaknesses remain and so on. But if we do keep notes, and use them to check on the accuracy of our memories over several months, we will probably get a shock. Eventually, with these notes, we will have quite a good map of each student's progress. If we still feel a little rudderless and wonder whether we are losing our sense of what had better be called 'public' standards, we can always show a range of essays to an interested colleague and ask him for a frank opinion on them and on our marking.

All these may well seem like counsels of perfection. But each has been followed by some tutors, and the best tutors I have seen have done all these things and more for much of the time. But some of us do hardly any of these things any of the time – because, in Britain, it is regarded as unnecessary or 'square' to think about the practice of good teaching. Our characteristic amateurism here is inexcusable.

Further reading

HIGHET, G. *The art of teaching* Methuen, 1951.
RICHARDS, I. A. *Interpretation in teaching* K. Paul, 1938.
HOGGART, R. *Speaking to each other* Vol. 2 About literature. Chatto, Oct. 1969.

TECHNIQUES OF DISCUSSION
by Geoffrey R. Brown

Every sort of adult teaching is improved by good class discussion, but developing and maintaining it is a skill that needs to be carefully thought out and practised. How can the tutor start people talking? What can he do about the people who talk too much? Some answers to these and other questions are suggested by Geoffrey R. Brown who is Tutor in Philosophy at the University of Oxford Delegacy for Extra Mural Studies.

In the context of adult education, discussion should be a genuinely shared conversation between members of a group or class. In this chapter I am concerned to present the case for such conversation as an important element in adult learning, to suggest ways in which it may be promoted and maintained and to discuss certain problems which may arise. My treatment is elementary in the sense that I have in mind basic points which I believe apply to all discussion in whatever particular adult education context it happens to take place. I assume, therefore, that there is a common experience which may be shared by tutors, whether they teach crafts, arts or academic subjects and whether they are primarily concerned with practical skills, creative imagination, aesthetic judgment or intellectual skills and understanding. At the end of this chapter, I have, however, suggested further reading dealing with the place of discussion in different contexts and subjects.

The case for discussion

If the question is put – why the need for a genuinely shared conversation? – it hardly seems to need an answer. But the general case is this. Adult learning is not primarily passive reception of the tutor's authoritative exposition but active involvement and participation in the matter which is to hand. Discussion is one means of securing such involvement and participation. The usual learning/teaching situation in adult education is a group situation and group discussion is one way of using this situation to educational advantage. It allows questions to be asked, positions to be challenged, ideas to be explored. It makes possible a variety of opinion; it makes public the openness of many questions; it may result in the sparking off of new ideas. Such discussion may serve as a check on the tutor and, in turn, may help him to assess the effectiveness of his teaching. Ability to discuss is itself a useful skill and can only be learned by entering into discussion. Further, discussion may be one means of transforming a collection of individuals, strangers to each other, into a friendly and co-operative group and this, in turn, makes for both enjoyment and better learning.

But I must not overstate the case. There are many queries. Is discussion the major way in which adults learn? Is it the only means of student participation? It may be crucial for the subjects where understanding is the goal and talk the main activity (e.g. philosophy) but is it really relevant to those subjects where the point is the learning of practical skills (e.g. cookery, pottery, woodwork)? It may be workable in a small group faced with a common problem and plenty of time, but is it really feasible in a large group where individuals are at different stages, where the emphasis is on individual work and time is short?

These doubts and queries are real enough. Discussion is certainly not the only method of learning, or necessarily the main method or always an applicable method. The local historian may stress field work, the archaeologist the dig, the biologist the laboratory experiment, the craft teacher the individual practical work – not, of course, to the exclusion of discussion for discussion can effectively be related to these alternatives, but as equally viable forms of student participation. There are, shall I say, a hundred-and-one methods and techniques and the good tutor will be concerned with a rich variety of methods and with judging which method or combination of methods is appropriate to the material and to the needs of the students. Exposition, demonstration, reading, writing, individual tasks, group performance, project, visit – all are possibilities. So discussion should be seen as a possibility – to be used when it would seem to be the most effective method.

On the face of it discussion may seem more effective in some subjects than others. Philosophy lends itself to immediate discussion in a way not possible with history or astronomy. The craft teacher may feel he has no need for group discussion; his class can function by demonstration, individual supervision and individual practice. People do not learn how to cook by talking about it. But, whatever the subject, it is a mistake for a tutor to dismiss discussion out of hand as automatically inapplicable. 'Teaching car maintenance is not all exposition and instruction by the teacher. Discussion plays an important part. One teacher writes that "through group discussion I have been able to formulate a syllabus that meets the requirements of students that attend my courses".' (Styler, W. E., *Further Education – Part-time Teachers Speak*, p. 29.) And some of the need for individual supervision in craft classes may be eliminated if certain problems are raised in general discussion following a demonstration or exposition.

But it has to be admitted that circumstances – shortage of time, size of class, differential progress of students – sometimes conspire to limit the possibilities of group discussion. The woodwork teacher may say that 'group teaching is very difficult with a practical subject like woodwork. Whatever group or class teaching is arranged it has to be supplemented by a good deal of individual teaching. Often a whole variety of different operations are in progress and the teacher can attend to only one student at a time.' (Styler, p. 26.) Even in this case it may be worth while for the tutor to promote general discussion from time to time as a means of relating individual performance and of sharing common problems. General group discussion might be just the way of mediating between the need for group teaching and the pressure for individual attention.

With these qualifications in mind, perhaps the fairest conclusion is that although group discussion may not always be central in all kinds of adult education, it has many advantages and the tutor should try to encourage it whenever it makes sense to do so. And it makes sense whenever the teaching and learning of a subject or skill involve (i) substantial chunks of exposition or demonstration by the tutor and/or (ii) evaluation, appraisal, critical examination and/or (iii) problem-solving. Discussion will reveal how much of the first has been understood and it will encourage the sharing of opinions so valuable for the second and third. And what teaching and learning worthy of the name does not at some time involve at least one of these?

The conduct of discussion

The case for discussion assumes, naturally, that when discussion takes place it will be effective. But what exactly is an 'effective' or a 'good' discussion? Perhaps the simplest answer is that a discussion is good if it achieves its particular end (or aim, goal, purpose . . .), e.g. the problem is solved. If there is no one particular end, a discussion is good if it achieves something of educational value, e.g. new insights, change of view, stimulation to further exploration, realisation of the complexity of a problem.

How then does the tutor promote and maintain this agreeable state of affairs? (In what follows I have in mind a fairly solid discussion lasting for some time and the sort of class where discussion is more central than peripheral. But I believe the points are applicable to other situations and classes.)

The environment in which the discussion takes place is an important factor in determining its effectiveness. Ideally, the room should not be too big for the number of people in the class and the seating arrangement should consist of a circle of chairs or a hollow square of desks so that, at the very least, class members can talk to each other directly, and the tutor is not, as it were, out on a limb. Perhaps the best is the hollow square of desks: there is something to put a book on, rest notes on or just lean on from time to time. Tutors will not always find such ideal conditions (an understatement). But they should try as best they can to create them. One of my classes meets in a typical school-room. Every week we rearrange the desks, etc., to form a square (and at the end, put them back). This takes both time and energy but I believe it is worth it in terms of effective discussion.

The above suggestions apply particularly to those classes where discussion is the staple diet. Other classes may have to arrange the furniture differently to fit in with the existing placing of machinery or apparatus or to facilitate individual work. But, even here, when exposition and discussion do take place it is better to get people to-gether – and around a focal point – than have them scattered at some distance from each other.

There is no ideal number of people for an effective discussion – situations vary and there are so many other factors involved. The literature of small group research contains many studies which try to relate size of group and group effectiveness but, unfortunately, the groups are seldom like those normally found in adult education in this country. In terms of discussion groups three points seem reasonably certain. The best size for a group varies with the task confronting it, e.g. with simple problem-solving very small groups may be as effective as larger groups but the more complex the task the more effective the larger group. But the larger the group the more uneven is participation in discussion; a few people tend to dominate discussion and the majority contribute little. And people tend to prefer groups which are neither very small nor very large: eight might be too small, above fifteen or sixteen too large.

A suitable environment and the right number of people will go a long way in helping a discussion to be effective. But they are not sufficient: discussion needs preparation. This does not mean that spontaneous discussion must be excluded. On the contrary, a discussion will often spring up in the adult class for which no one is strictly prepared but which is obviously so important and germane that the tutor will do all he can to encourage it. Nor does it mean that every discussion has to be carefully programmed, follow a set pattern, keep to the exact topic laid down, always come to a conclusion. But it does mean that *usually* both tutor *and* student should prepare for the discussion.

There are any number of ways of preparing for – and being prepared for – discussion. The tutor may introduce a given topic by exposition, he may demonstrate a technique, he may use visual aids. This is preparation for discussion in the sense that there is then something on which to bite. But more important is the student's own preparatory work. A student may prepare a paper which he presents to the class; all students may read around a given topic before the discussion or write papers on different aspects of the question to be discussed; all students may have copies of the relevant material (e.g. a poem) which they have already read and thought about; the students may already be prepared by their individual practical work to discuss common problems. Preparatory work is best linked with discussion if it (i) suggests a clear problem to be tackled, poses a definite issue, presents a basic question (this means that the problem/issue/question must be discussable, relevant and open – it must *not* be too wide, obviously factual, uncontroversial, artificially imposed by the tutor or apparently already answered in the preparation) and (ii) provides a common basis of knowledge related to the problem or a shared experience out of which the problem – and therefore the discussion – naturally arises.

Linking preparatory work and discussion should have a double effect. Discussion should be an incentive to do the preparatory reading etc., and the preparation should make for better discussion.

In the end, however favourable the environment and however

thorough the preparation the effectiveness of a discussion depends on how it is actually carried out. Suppose a tutor has to take a class in a given subject over twelve or twenty-four weeks and discussion is going to play a part in the class. The first few meetings are particularly important. On the first evening people (including the tutor) may confront each other as strangers; and there may be no preparation to fall back on. The tutor will be concerned at that meeting and in the immediately following meetings to create a friendly and confident group; to find out what people want and need; to set people working. Some discussion will be useful in promoting all three aims, whether the subject is academic or strictly practical. Part of the discussion might well be concerned with finding out what people already know and how this relates to what they want (e.g. the Car Maintenance class) or with building up a scheme of work on the basis of shared views. Discussion may also follow the first demonstration or exposition by the tutor. He must be prepared for silence, uncertainty, slowness. Discussion will need encouragement. People may not know quite what to expect, what they are supposed to do. They may be nervous. They may find the class more demanding than they thought. The tutor must allow people time to respond, to build up confidence, to express their opinions and state their interests, and to react to other people's opinions and interests. Over the weeks following the first meeting discussion should become a matter of course along with the other class activities appropriate to the particular subject being studied.

The tutor need not conduct every particular discussion session in the same way. There are in fact many possibilities. Here are two examples.

Not every discussion has to begin with a tutor's exposition. If the class is already well prepared, e.g. they are to discuss a poem which they have all read, and about which they have all thought, there is no point in the tutor beginning with a long talk. It will be better to proceed immediately to the discussion. Here the unifying element is not a single question or problem but shared material and/or experience. The discussion is not built around the clarification and exploration of a basic question but the exploration of basic material and response to that material. There may be no obvious order which the discussion ought to follow. The tutor may begin by inviting people to state their reactions. Out of these statements there may spring two or three crucial questions. The class may discuss which are the important questions and go on to discuss them. Gradually significant points may emerge. The tutor may find that all he would have said is, in fact, being said in the discussion. The points he would have made in exposition are instead arising naturally and meaningfully in the context of a cumulative conversation.

Or again a class may begin with each member being given a duplicated list of questions or a tick-off sheet (yes/no alternatives) centred on a given topic. He is asked to complete the sheet and (possibly) to write down in brief the reason for his answers or choices. Each member has thus committed himself privately in terms of his own experience. The questions on the sheet then form the basis for group discussion where members can share their opinions publicly. Gradually a more complex picture is built up around the topic and the really serious issues are pinpointed and discussed. This method may be particularly useful where students have a good deal of personal experience which needs to be brought to bear systematically on a given topic, e.g. trades unionists discussing the role of the shop steward or the purposes of collective bargaining.

There is no point in multiplying examples; further variations and possibilities suggest themselves – discussion emanating from role-playing, discussion as part of a case-study, class television viewing/discussion. Which method or methods a tutor decides to use will depend on a host of factors but he should at least be aware of the possibilities.

Because there are so many possibilities it follows that the tutor has no fixed role to play in all kinds of discussions. He is sometimes the *authority* and sometimes *just one of the members of the class*. But he must not always act the authority and it is silly for him to pretend he is always just a class member. His role will be determined by the particular kind of discussion the class is engaged in. In fact he must be prepared to fill many roles. He may be *organiser* when he arranges for the duplication of background material for the industrial relations class. He may be *initiator*, e.g. the craft teacher deliberately arranges his demonstration so that discussion about it seems the most natural thing in the world. He may be *chairman* – 'Have we covered this point adequately?'. He may be *adviser* or *consultant* when he takes no part in the case-study discussion but is there to be consulted if necessary. In certain circumstances he may be *gadfly*. If he finds that members of the class can fill some or all of these roles from time to time he should encourage them to do so. One may collect material for the discussion, another may start the discussion, a third may have the knowledge and experience to act as a consultant on a particular issue, all may carry out quite informally the functions of chairman. And most classes have their gadfly.

But, most important, the tutor must be careful not to interpret his roles in such a way that he himself makes effective discussion impossible. If he initiates discussion he must not spend too long over it. If he acts as consultant, he must restrain himself until consulted. If he acts as chairman he must *not* directly answer every question raised, decide always what is to be discussed or what is the point at issue, cut people off, intervene when people are still thinking. He must not talk too much. If he expects good discussion he must himself obey the rules. He must be both tolerant and patient. He must not be afraid to let the discussion go and not too anxious to resume control. He must count it a success if class members cease to speak automatically to and through him but address their remarks directly to each other.

When the tutor is actually engaged in a discussion he will have to decide many questions of detail. Should he be pushing the discussion towards a conclusion because time is short? Would a break from discussion be a good thing? The discussion is lagging because a vital question has not been raised or essential information for a new question is lacking – should he raise the question, inject the information or should he wait a little to see if it comes up from the group? Suppose there is no discussion. How long can he wait for it? Suppose someone is asserting falsehoods as facts or putting forward really outrageous, ridiculous or prejudiced opinions? Does he immediately correct or check? Does he wait for someone else to do it for him. Suppose this does not happen. . . .

There can be no firm answers to this kind of question but a few suggestions may be of use. On the whole the tutor should not push a discussion towards a conclusion. This would defeat the point of the exercise and would be false to the spirit of open discussion. But if a group is engaged on a problem which *can* have an answer, it may be frustrating to have to break off a discussion without having settled something – then the tutor may push. A break in the middle of a long discussion is often a good thing – people may come back refreshed. When discussion lags or fails, the tutor will often find it pays not to step in too quickly. It may be a pause for breath rather than a complete collapse. If discussion has really petered out he should move on to something new rather than attempt a revival. If after his exposition or demonstration there is simply no discussion the fault is more likely to be in the exposition/demonstration than the class and the remedy can only be a rethinking of his approach. If falsehoods go unchecked and opinions pass unopposed the tutor has the duty of putting the record straight and of stating the counter-opinions – for this, of course, is the expertise he has to offer the group. But he must at the same time give his sources, or the evidence or the arguments.

These questions show very clearly that a tutor's conduct of discussion is not just a matter of technique; it is essentially a matter of judgment. And perhaps more important than either technique or judgment are certain qualities of enthusiasm and honesty . . .

Problems

Anyone who has ever taken part in discussions will know that there are certain standard problems – irrelevance, wandering off the point, the very talkative person, the silent person, the person who because of expertise dominates a discussion, the person who feels he has nothing to contribute, the discussion which fails to get anywhere because there are too many people involved.

Stock situations of irrelevance easily spring to mind. A discussion is going well and someone introduces a personal reminiscence or story which seems quite unconnected with the point at issue. Someone with a bee in his bonnet tries to turn discussion towards a question which is more amenable to his own purposes and knowledge. Or a whole discussion may gradually be getting away from the point. The tutor has to be careful in assessing whether something is really relevant or not. What a person says or a group does is not relevant or irrelevant in itself but only within a given context, namely, the question or problem which is the point of the discussion. And even then relevance is a matter of degree. What seems to be irrelevant might in fact be an original way of looking at the question at issue; what looks irrelevant may lead to something highly relevant if pursued. For these reasons the tutor must be tolerant of what he takes to be irrelevance. Sometimes the group will spot when they are getting away from the point and someone will query whether they are still discussing the question at issue. The tutor himself may sometimes have to raise the question of whether they are wandering off the point. He may have to re-state the question at issue more carefully: sometimes irrelevance is caused by haziness as to what the question at issue is; a clearly defined focal point will help to maintain relevance and make it easier for people to spot irrelevance.

Many people like to talk and if they did not discussion could hardly begin. But some people are rather persistent talkers. They tend to take more than their fair share of the discussion. There is the man who always jumps in first and at length, the compulsive arguer, the man who talks sense at length, the man who is irrelevant at length (not only men, of course). Each can be a problem: the man who talks sense at great length may be just as destructive of real discussion as the long-winded persistently irrelevant person. Yet the tutor should not be over-anxious. He does not have to stop everyone who speaks longer than two minutes. He does not have to worry if some people express themselves briefly and others take more time about it. But he does have to judge whether – in a given context – a person is really 'hogging it' too much. If he judges that this is the case and that it may become persistent unless checked, there are various things he may do. He may rely on the other members of the class to keep the talker within reasonable time limits. He may use humour – a joke – to bring home to the member that he is stealing too much of the available time. He may stop the talker and say that because he is making so many points the class had better take up one immediately and then ask what other people think about that *one* point. He may have to have a tactful private word with the offender.

Most people in adult classes do say something but there will usually be one or two people who say little or nothing. They may be following the discussion with keen interest but prefer to go over it in their heads rather than contribute. They may indeed be ahead of the discussion but they do not want to step in and kill it. Or they may be shy, feel they have nothing to say, do not want to make fools of themselves. They may be a little out of their depth, not quite following what is going on. There are many possible reasons why students may stay silent in a discussion. Nor is silence necessarily a bad thing. A good discussion does not entail that everyone must speak or be forced to speak on any given occasion or that all speak for the same length of time. But if a class member is persistently silent the tutor must be prepared to do something about it, not just for the sake of group discussion – he must be very careful not to manipulate individuals for the sake of group ends – but to make sure that the member benefits from his attendance at the class. The tutor must make sure that the silent student really does know he is free to speak and does feel that his contribution is wanted. He should make it clear that all contributions are valuable. He may help the student by finding out if he has some special experience about which he can be persuaded to speak. He must seize the chance of a private word to discover if the student is following the discussion and finding the course useful. During a discussion he may direct a question to the student or ask for his opinion – but he must be very careful here for obvious reasons. The tutor can perhaps take comfort from the fact that silent members often become less silent over time and, in any case, those who speak least often make good contributions in other ways.

It is rare for the adult class to contain more than one or two members who are problems because of their extreme loquacity or their persistent silence. But it is not rare for classes to be very mixed, to contain people of different ages, occupations, education, experience, and general background. This can be an advantage. A philosophy class with men and women, an age-range from twenty to over sixty, and including a casual worker, a surveyor, several teachers, a zoologist and two mathematicians makes for an interesting variety of opinion in discussion. But there can also be problems. A class may contain members representing extremes in educational background or practical skill. How can they discuss together in a way that is profitable to each ? The obvious and simplest solution is to remove the problem by deliberately separating classes as elementary, intermediate or advanced. This is the practice in language teaching and in much craft teaching and it may be growing in industrial relations teaching where there are often basic and advanced courses. Or the problem may be circumvented by the deliberate encouragement of more homogeneous groups derived from a single professional interest. But in much of adult education these solutions are neither possible nor desirable. The tutor will still be faced with a heterogeneous class.

This is not the place to discuss all the ways in which a class may be mixed and how each may be a problem. Take just one example. Suppose a class contains three or four people who are relatively expert in respect of the subject to be studied and other people who are relative beginners. It is clear what may happen. The experts may dominate discussion and if prevented from doing so may become bored with its pace. The beginners may become interested spectators feeling at the same time that they have nothing to contribute. The tutor's problem is first to control the experts. He must not allow the class to become a conversation between himself and them. He must

77

not allow them to cut other people out. He must not allow them to subtly control the direction of discussion. He will need firmness; his role as chairman will be much in evidence. But he must also maintain the experts' interest while he encourages the beginners. In my experience this is less hard than it might seem. The majority in a class may be beginners but this does not mean that discussion has to be simple. It is the oversimplified treatment which bores the expert not the serious exploration of an elementary question. At the same time the beginner is encouraged when he grasps the elementary question and may feel impelled to contribute to its exploration.

The tutor may find himself taking a class whose numbers are really too large for effective discussion. The usual practice is lecture and questions or, if the subject allows, the carrying out of individual tasks with supervision. But discussion may be possible by the method of breaking down the large audience into several fairly small groups. An example will illustrate the possibilities.

On a particular evening the problem for the politics class is how the ordinary citizen of a given area may seek to influence or change a central government decision affecting the area. The tutor has already prepared four short documents, each document summarising a different case-study or outlining a possible problem situation relevant to the topic for discussion. He divides his large class into four groups, gives each group one of the documents and asks them to discuss their particular case-study or work out what they would do in response to their particular problem. After perhaps half an hour the groups reassemble as a class, each group reports on its discussion, the reports are compared and general implications brought out.

I said at the beginning of this chapter that I would be concerned with certain general points about discussion. But there is a limit to such general talk. More specific accounts of the place of discussion in the rich variety of adult education situations and subjects may be found in the following list of books and articles.

Further reading

PETERSON, A. D. C., ed. *Techniques of teaching* Vol. 3 Tertiary education. Pergamon P., 1965.

BUREAU OF CURRENT AFFAIRS *Discussion method* Dobson, 1952.

STYLER, W. E. *Further education: part-time teachers speak* Univ. of Hull, Dept. of Adult Education, 1968.

STYLER, W. E. *Questions and discussion* Workers' Educational Assoc. 1952.

HOGGART, R. Notes on extra-mural teaching in *Adult Education* Vol. 33, no. 3, pp. 105–9 and no. 4, pp. 178–82, 1960.

NATIONAL INSTITUTE OF ADULT EDUCATION *Methods at Holly Royde*; by R. D. Waller. The Inst., 1965.

ROBINSON, J. and BARNES, N., eds. *New media and methods in industrial training* BBC, 1968.

EDUCATION AND SCIENCE, Dept. of, University Grants Committee. *Report of the Committee on university teaching methods* (Hale report). H.M.S.O., 1964.

PARSONS, D. Discovery learning in archaeology in *Adult Education* Vol. 41, no. 4, 1968, pp. 241–9.

STUART, D. G. and WATTS, N. Class television viewing – two experiments in *Adult Education* Vol. 40, no. 4, 1967, pp. 237–44.

MARRIOTT, S. Student-centred teaching in *Adult Education* Vol. 40, no. 4, 1967, pp. 232–7.

KLEIN, J. *Working with groups* Hutchinson, 1966.

JAMES, W. Group dynamics theories in *Adult Education* Vol. 37, nos. 3 and 4, 1964.

EXTENDING THE SUBJECT
by George Whittle

How can a teacher extend his subject and his students so that educational boundaries are broadened? George Whittle, Inspector of Further Education for Birmingham, describes a number of ways in which he has seen the teaching of a skill developed into a rich and satisfying educational process.

The title refers to Programme 5 which looked particularly at the work of craft teachers and asked how far their responsibility should go beyond teaching the basic techniques of the craft into consideration of aesthetics, design and social values. It also raised the question of this broadening principle for other than craft teachers.

The title is misleading. 'Extending the Student' would be more appropriate. The teacher's task is education – developing and cultivating the physical, intellectual and moral faculties of the student and to do this he must extend the student. He starts from the initial interests and declared needs of the students and from this often dull and unpromising beginning, extends and helps them to discover new areas of knowledge, new depths of understanding and wider horizons of interests and so develop unrealised potential in themselves. The subject and the subject skills are a means to this end and the initial interest in the subject is the tool with which the teacher begins.

'Not subject knowledge, but personal progress towards human excellence is the criterion of adult eduction.' (H.M. Staff Inspector J. A. Simpson.)

We would see this more clearly if we used the German title for adult education – *Volksbildung* – which might roughly be translated 'people-building', for it reminds us that our task is people not subject orientated and we must extend the subject to extend the student.

However lofty our aims we can only begin where our students are, at the point of conscious need and interest which has brought them to the class. In the main, people come to Adult Education classes, especially those provided by Local Education Authorities, because they want to do things (sing, pot, paint), to make things (tables, dresses, lampshades), to learn something (a language, sail a boat, invest money). These are the most readily declared motives and they may express an underlying desire for a sense of achievement, personal and social competence. There is in many also a need for friendship, and the fellowship of the group, and some have cultural motives arising from a belief in the intrinsic value of certain subjects. For the majority of those who join craft classes, the needs and the motives seem immediate and practical – to make and to do – and unless they have convincing evidence right early in the course that these needs will be met they will 'vote with their feet' and we will have no further opportunity to help them towards 'personal excellence', or any other of our worthy educational ideals. Our first task then is to help the student to learn the skill, meet the need, accomplish the task, solve the problem that brought him to the class. Here begins our opportunity to extend the student to levels of achievement, interest, knowledge and understanding, of which he never thought himself capable or even knew existed.

This is the point of view that Programme 5 explored. We saw teachers of craft subjects who demonstrated that their job is not only a matter of teaching skills but that there are wider possibilities. The programme did, however, leave an impression with some viewing groups that the teaching of skills and techniques was regarded as second-class education, or perhaps not even education at all. Some viewers I know thought the programme was saying that the real education did not begin until the student could be taken into the wider possibilities where, for example, the soft furnishing group discussed 'design or perhaps period furniture'. We need, therefore, to remind ourselves that in exploring and mastering new skills the student is intellectually, physically, and morally challenged and developed, no more or less than if he were engaged in so-called intellectual pursuits. '. . . the standards of the craftsman and the artist are not to be despised. They too have the power to release the energies of the timid, to stretch the mind, and to discipline the proud.' (H. J. Edwards, *The Evening Institute*.)

The tragedy is that so much of the doing and making in adult education craft groups is dull and repetitive with little or no challenge or extension of the student. Walter James weighed up the situation nicely in his discussion with the producer of *Teaching Adults*, Roger Owen.

Walter James 'It isn't that they should not embroider Victorian Ladies on cushions, but once they know how to do Victorian Ladies on cushions they can go away and do it for the rest of their lives. They do not need an educational institution and they do not need a teacher paid by a local authority in order that they can do that. . . . It is not something for an educational activity which should be stretching them and making them aware of a whole range of possibilities which in their ordinary life and without a teacher they might not be aware of.'

Roger Owen 'There are some subjects, popular in evening institutes, e.g. Ballroom Dancing, in which the aim of the students is to master a technique – to dance the slow fox-trot in the way the slow fox-trot should be danced. Is this an educational activity?'

Walter James 'Yes, like every skill it should be taught. Once taught, once practised, once part of a person, then there is no further need for it as an educational activity. It can become a social activity, it can be a recreational activity.'

The basic aim of the craft class is the teaching and learning of skills and in so far as this extends the student, and aids his physical, mental, and moral development, it is a valid educational activity. In the process, however, there arise naturally a host of opportunities to enrich the educational value of the activity – opportunities which lead the student into new areas of knowledge and understanding of which he might not become aware without the help of a teacher alert to the possibilities.

H.M. Staff Inspector J. A. Simpson, in his paper on 'Good Teaching', suggested that 'We have a right to expect the use of every opportunity to make people not only better linguists, or cooks, or car owners, but more thoughtful, knowledgeable, critical human beings, with wider horizons.' He went on to mention ways in which the subject could be generally educative – 'whether it be Car Maintenance or Dressmaking, or whatever.'

'(a) It can do much to enhance the students' general powers of choice, discrimination, judgment, ability to see relationships and sense of what is aesthetically fitting.

'(b) It can suggest analogies between its own specific principles of technique and those of other aspects of life – such principles as economy of effort or material, elegance and sound design.

'(c) It can widen horizons through its own subject science or history or experimental development, as with the chemistry of nylon. It is sad when a class in Italian never hears of Dante. I was gladdened to visit a German Class last year listening to a recorded Goethe poem. And what of Gibbons or Sheraton in Woodwork, Sèvres and Meissen in pottery, Brillat Savarin in cuisine.'

Increasingly teachers in Adult Education Classes have become aware of the need and the opportunity for making their subjects more generally educative in these ways. The teacher who appeared with her flower arranging class, said of her students, 'I know they only came to learn to put flowers into water. . . . I hope that through my subject I can persuade them to branch out into all sorts of exciting activities.' So as well as a demonstration, and practice of arrangements, the class had a lively, well-illustrated five-minute talk on baskets, the containers used for the arrangement. This lively interlude ranged quickly from birds' nests to Moses, Isaiah, Coracles, Victoriana and 'pop baskets'. Here was a teacher using a natural take-off point within her subject to widen the mental horizon of her students and spark off new interests. The dressmaking teacher broke into the buzz of individual activities in her class for what appeared to be a bit of incidental teaching, to show and describe 'Zenana Cloth'. An Indian student explained the meaning of the word Zenana (ladies). I know that after the demonstration there were lots of questions, and intelligent critical discussion about women in India and Indian women in Birmingham. The other dressmaking teacher in the programme widened the interest of her students from the craft of making a dress to a wider consideration of dress by bringing into the classroom an exhibition of 'up-to-the-minute clothes from a local boutique'. One can well imagine the discussion on fashion and style, built-in obsolescence, etc. that this might stimulate.

These examples from the programme illustrate ways of widening the horizon of the student. This is probably the most popular and easily applied area for extending the subject. More numerous and profitable are the natural opportunities that occur, especially in craft subjects, for education in choice and judgment, and in the power to discriminate, but more often these opportunities are missed and the activity becomes repetitive, nothing more than the students doing what they were told.

Roger Owen 'In other words people learn *how* to do things. *Why* things should be done in one way rather than another, or whether they should be done at all, these are the kind of questions which tend to be pushed to one side. The women we saw learning about make-up were a case in point; questions of individual taste and judgment were not raised. This is the way it is done. This is the way it has got to be done. Off you go and do it.'

For the instructor, fair enough, but the educator winces at the waste of such golden opportunities for enhancing the students' general powers of choice, and a sense of what is aesthetically fitting. By contrast Alison Erridge, in the training of teachers of dress and embroidery, shows how we can help teachers to make the most of their opportunities to lead their students on beyond the teaching of techniques to more generally educative areas where the skill can be allied to judgment, taste, creativity and good design. As she put it, 'What we are trying to do now is to produce a generation of teachers who are first of all creatively trained, who can pry creativity out of their class . . . to educate them thoroughly enough technically, but leave them with a free enough mind, so that they can enlarge everybody's vision, improve everybody's work, without superimposing a set form or technique, or a set form of design on everybody . . . and to make them feel that what is personal and genuine is more important and more valuable than what is limited and hackneyed.' Teachers with this mind in them will find opportunities in almost any subject to enlarge the vision of their students by widening mental horizons, involving them in exercising judgment and discrimination by stirring their curiosity and enthusiasm; to question the old and explore the new. Many teachers, however, do not easily recognise these opportunities and have not developed the skills of seizing upon them. Let us then examine a few more ways and means of extending the subject and the student.

I visited an Ikebana group some months ago and spontaneously there arose an interesting discussion which ranged over Japanese art, cameras, motorcycles and religion. We explored the relationship between the precision in Japanese art, Japanese prowess in fine engineering, then to Shintoism, which as one student put it 'is a religion which put everyone in their place and order'. Every member of the group contributed and it was significant that the discussion took place after the flower arrangements had been completed. I came upon a class when they were evaluating various floral displays that they had arranged. This was a group able to make, and take, intelligent appraisal of their own work. The standard of communication was high, the discussion lively, and it seemed natural that someone should ask 'What is beauty?', and that the reply should come 'Beauty is truth, and truth beauty', and that like the 'Jesting Pilate' someone countered, 'What is truth?' A nun in the group took over at this point and I left. These students had no doubt come to 'Learn to put flowers into water' but were excited by the level of the discussion which followed, and enjoyed their improving powers of communication. Maybe this level of philosophical discussion is not within the range of every teacher's competence, but it must surely be expected that this subject will be extended to an interest in horticulture, painting, and other closely allied activities.

Car Maintenance students can very easily be led into the rich fields of intellectual training, starting from the economic motive which brings many of them to join the class. On our teacher-training courses we suggest that popular advertisements are a good starting point. Can it be true? Why should it cost more? Is it really better? What did *Which?* say about it? How did *Which?* carry out its investigation? I saw a very good lesson on batteries which began with the price range and advertising blurbs for batteries offered locally, including cut-price offers. Before the end of the evening there were very heated discussions about re-sale price maintenance; arguments which carried on into the coffee break and on to the pub after the meeting.

I once joined a woodwork class on a visit to a small Cotswold town and its furniture factory renowned for good design; a day full of interesting comment on sound design, elegance, the history of furniture, and economy of material and effort. Here the subject was extended far beyond the learning of skills and beyond the classroom. I cannot see how a teacher of woodwork can fail to share his enthusiasm for wood and furniture with his students, and the metalwork teacher his delight in a precise, well-designed piece of engineering. These are things that are caught, not taught. Fortunately most of our Woodwork and Metalwork classes take place in rooms where there are plenty of illustrations, displays and models, which easily start off conversations which widen mental horizons and raise questions of taste and judgment. The teacher's work and jobs being done by the 'day-school lads' are first-class starting points, especially if they are displayed strategically and the teacher can spontaneously draw attention to them in his obvious enthusiasm.

Dressmaking is another one of those subjects it seems impossible not to extend, and an interest in making a dress would seem almost naturally to lead to consideration of current fashions, fabrics, sensible shopping, planning an outfit, grooming, taste, colour and design. Alert and informed teachers have dozens of chances, arising incidentally at each meeting, to interest and inform their students in these topics. Any teacher worth her salt should be able to entertain her group with a short discussion on any of these interests, especially if she is equipped with the appropriate visual aids. Displays of books and magazines lead the students to explore the topics on their own and libraries are usually eager to forge links between classes and the local library. Dress parades and exhibitions arranged by, and for, the members seem to be the most natural extenders, and especially if the members are involved in the planning of the operation.

I liked Walter James' idea for an experimental cookery class where, after the grammar of cookery had been learned, students are encouraged to experiment, to create new dishes not bound by traditional recipes but to use their own imagination and judgment, trying different flavours, different quantities, to produce new and exciting dishes. 'Human beings develop by constant exploration,' he said, 'by curiosity, by not being satisfied by what they have previously found out, by wanting to find out the new and explore the new.' Cookery classes which seem to offer merely instruction in basic skills are now, I think, losing their appeal. Adults want a wider more adventurous approach to the subject. Food Education rather than Cookery is what is needed with a widening of interest to include diets (especially for slimming), sensible shopping and simple entertaining. Slimming seems a natural lead for any cookery class into a study of food values and value for money. In one of our Institutes a group of cookery classes carried their consumer education a stage further by combining for a short course on 'Meat Appeal'. No doubt the master butcher who demonstrated had some valuable consumer education also. Cookery classes find it very easy to extend their interest by combining with other groups in the Centre to cater for social functions. Cookery, Flower Arrangement and Wine-Making is a very natural combination which provided a widening of horizons for all concerned and a good deal of judgment, choice and discrimination in the planning of a party. The teacher of cookery often has to start from the glamorous and adventurous and extend backwards as it were to cover the basic skills and basic facts about nutrition – the reverse of the usual situation. Cookery classes linked with television series have had plenty of opportunity to do just this.

The why and how of extending the subject and the students have been illustrated by referring to practical subjects, but the same principles and methods would seem to apply to a wide range of classes. In the more traditionally academic subjects, extensions arise easily and attempts to explore the wider possibilities meet with less resistance from staff and students. All the adult language classes I have known have gone easily into considerations of the country and the people. Posters, films, slides, records, tapes, visits, newspapers, magazines, scattered liberally through the adult education language class provide easy access to discussions on geography, economics, politics, especially if they are provided by members to illustrate accounts of their own experiences. The subjects in the R.B. (Extra-Mural and W.E.A.) prospectuses lend themselves readily to the liberalisation, which Staff Inspector J. A. Simpson has defined as 'the liberation of mind, that enhanced capacity to judge, that sound order of values which is the ultimate aim of all education'. Even so, the R.B. tutor must be challenged to inquire if his group is as outward-looking as we expect the L.E.A. craft class to be. Could his students not be more extended by engaging in some local social survey, compiling a local history and arranging an appropriate exhibition, or similar activities ? How far is his teaching limited to giving facts and how far does it involve the students in solving problems, asking questions, how, why and if? Projects, case-studies, role-playing, problem-solving, these are the methods by which it would seem he can most naturally extend his students, but there may be something for him to learn from the tactics employed by the craft teachers.

Teachers of technical training and vocational subjects cannot escape their responsibility to use opportunities to make the students 'more thoughtful, knowledgeable critical human beings' by using natural breaks to extend the subject. It is indeed a rich bonus if we can teach the trainee not only to make and do but also help him towards wider mental horizons and an enhanced capacity to judge, which comes from a liberal treatment of the subject. After all, the techniques we are teaching will probably be outmoded in ten years but the capacity to judge and the versatile mind which are the products of good liberal education will never be obsolete. One of our best part-time teachers of Shorthand and Typewriting can always, it seems, find time to leaven her teaching with a little liberalisation. When dealing with a passage about Lloyds Insurance there was a lively discussion on the people who could afford to join by guaranteeing £50,000 and investing a further £15,000 in stocks and securities. How did they make their money? What did they get out of it? Passages for dictation or transcription are carefully chosen to provide opportunities for liberal education. The attendance is very good, the wastage low, the examination results well above average because the students find the class lively, attractive and extending.

There is one method of extending the subject that deserves special mention; the short residential course. In the relaxed and friendly residential atmosphere students seem very eager and willing to explore the more liberal aspects of their subjects. As one woman put it, 'somehow it is releasing and I don't mind so much trying new methods and new things'. Drama and Opera Groups are ready to step off the treadmill of production and study costume, movement, voice production, etc. Dressmakers and Homecrafters are willing to consider colour and design, and Cooks consumer education. Some of the successful courses provided by one of our Birmingham Institutes, which serves a not very salubrious area, have included 'Protecting the Consumer', 'Photography in Everyday Life', 'The Age of the Motor Car' in which teachers and students studied together to extend themselves and their subjects.

I feel that I may have made it all sound too easy, especially for the teacher of practical subjects, and that I have tempted the unwary to dash off and make enthusiastic, but clumsy efforts which might empty their classes. There are barriers which teachers must overcome before they can extend their students beyond the learning of the basic techniques in adult education craft classes. The students want early evidence that the primary objectives for which they joined the course will be achieved in minimal time. They will not tolerate dull, long-winded, apparently irrelevant time-consuming diversions. The extension can only take place within the limits of the students' tolerance and in the early stages of the course, at least, the extension must be approached informally, incidentally, arising naturally from the job in hand. There is a misconception that extending the subject inevitably means 'stop what you are doing, gather round me and listen'. Until the teacher is experienced and a firm friendly relationship established with the group, the extension will have to come much more spontaneously than that. In every situation, however, there are opportunities for decision-making, for asking the questions 'What is our problem? How do we solve it? Have we got the solution?' This is the basis of good general education. The biggest barriers are, I suspect, the limitations of the teacher outside his technical expertise. Much depends upon his own breadth of outlook, depth of understanding, and teaching skill.

There is plenty we can do to remove the limitations of teachers who are not equipped to teach their subject liberally or to extend the student beyond the learning of the basic techniques of the subject. First of all, at our staff selection we must be looking for people who have wide mental horizons and whose outlook shows evidence of their own good general liberal education. Should we appoint anyone to teach Ikebana who does not have a good knowledge of Japan and its people and products? It seems to me that in our selection and training of part-time teachers our concern has been too narrowly technical. (Alison Erridge expressed this very well in the passage quoted earlier in this chapter.) We must provide encouragement and opportunities for our craft teachers to extend their own general education, starting with topics in or around their own subject, e.g. an elementary course in the chemistry of man-made fibres for Dressmaking Teachers. In consultation with organisers at staff meetings and training courses, teachers should examine the tactics that have been successfully used to extend the subject. Furthermore they should be given facilities to watch successful practitioners at work, to see how the opportunities for extension arise naturally, especially in the designing and planning of articles to be made, projects to be undertaken, and from the natural curiosity of the students and the enthusiasm of the teacher. Above all we need to provide training in the skills of stimulating and conducting discussion, not only the short set-piece breaks, but more especially the exploration of talking points which crop up easily when people get together to pursue a common interest. This is the skill of drawing from adult students the considerable wealth of knowledge and experience they possess and helping them to stimulate each other to extend themselves.

People brought together in task-related groups in the appropriate environment, and given the right stimuli, will extend themselves and their interest in the subject. The role of the teacher is to provide this environment, and stimulus. He will, however, only be able to do this effectively if he knows and believes that his task is not primarily subject-teaching, but *Volksbindung*, and in this cause extends himself to extend the subject to extend the student.

Further reading

NATIONAL INSTITUTE OF ADULT EDUCATION *The evening institute*; by H. J. Edwards; The Inst., 1961.

TEACHING AS INVESTIGATION
by Maurice Broady

Many of the authors of these chapters have commented on the need to make teaching adults a process of active rather than passive learning; Professor Shaw and Mr Carter talk about how adult education can be involved in the whole community. In this chapter, Maurice Broady links these two themes by describing a kind of sociology teaching-by-project in which he and others have used active methods to investigate the community itself. He also discusses what general relevance projects have for all teachers of adults.

Maurice Broady is Senior Lecturer in Sociology at the University of Southampton.

A number of years ago, I had a suit made by one of the best tailors in Liverpool. It was a very good suit, of heavy blue hopsack, and it cost a lot of money. Now it happened that my father was a Manchester garment-maker and when I next saw him, I asked his opinion of this suit. He looked it carefully up and down, rubbed the cloth appraisingly between his finger and thumb and agreed that it was excellently tailored.

Why, I asked, *was* it a good suit? Well, he said, look at how the back drapes straight from the shoulders; look how snugly the lapels lie down on the chest; look how neatly the sleeves fit into the jacket. Yes, I continued, fascinated by my father's ability to explain what exactly, in his judgment, counted as a good coat: but how has that effect been achieved?

At this point, my father began to talk about things that the layman, like me, knew nothing about – about what lay *underneath* the well-fitting lapels and the straight drape. Underneath the lapel, for instance, was canvas and this canvas had been felled. As the tailor, stitch after stitch, had felled it he had pulled ever so slightly on the thread so as to give a tension to the canvas which, conveyed to the cloth, brought the lapel smooth and well-fitting on the breast. In much the same way, my father continued to explain the quality of the suit by referring to the tailoring techniques which were there but which the untutored eye did not and could not see. All at once, I realised how superficial was *my* judgment by comparison with my father's; and that he saw that jacket with the eye of one who had actually *made* coats and who understood the skill of the tailor's fingers that underlay what one saw on the surface.

It was this conversation which brought me to a way of thinking about sociology which has guided the practice of adult education that I shall go on to describe. Most people are not sociologists any more than they are tailors. But in the same way that most people wear a suit the tailor makes, so most people, some time or another, read a bit of sociology. It may be Young and Willmott's celebrated study of family life in the East End of London or Wright Mills' account of the American power élite. But most people, untutored in sociology as I was in tailoring, would merely be able to say of a sociological study – as I could say of the suit – 'Yes, that's good' or 'That's an awful book'.

The dangers of superficial and uninformed judgments where *ideas* or theories are concerned are, however, much greater, since what we *do* is governed by how we *think* and what we *understand*; and flabby thinking and uncritical understanding are often the seed-beds of social injustice and personal iniquity. The educational purpose of doing sociology with the layman must therefore be to develop his ability to judge the value of a sociological account with greater accuracy and skill. This can be done by reading such accounts critically. But we know that people learn best by doing something rather than by passively listening and that is why, in Extra-Mural teaching, the tutorial discussion – the close, direct engagement of students and tutor in argument – has always held a central place.

But another way of developing critical judgment is to engage directly in the process of actually fabricating knowledge. For it is experience in and reflection upon *this* process which makes it possible for the sociologist – or the historian or the physicist for that matter – to make the same kind of tight and incisive judgments that my father was able to make about that suit, out of a comparable experience in and reflection upon *his* craft. Thus, when I read a bit of sociology, page after page, I do it with an eye that is informed by years of making knowledge of that sort: of gathering the cloth of factual information, of making the pattern of theoretical conceptions, of cutting the information to meet the size of my problem, of tailoring the pieces of knowledge to fit the pattern of ideas and, finally, of sewing it all together with the thread of words so as to produce a well-argued book or account or critique. In my field, then, as in my father's, I came to appreciate that a genuine understanding came only from doing the job of making either a coat, or, in my case, a sociological argument.

Until the early sixties, however, while the adult teaching that I had done had always involved discussion, it had never involved students in the process of actually making knowledge. The standard kind of Extra-Mural class began with a lecture which would be followed by a discussion, together with some short pieces of written work done rather mechanically by the students. But there came the point, some ten years ago, when I had to experiment with another method.

The circumstances were the following. I had been asked to do sociology with a group of young people from a Glasgow day-release college. They had all done particularly well in their examinations and had been given the opportunity of spending a week at an adult education college in a Cumberland village. It was the first time that I had ever taken such a group; and it seemed clear that the standard practice of the lecture and discussion would not be suitable in these circumstances: that it would not do to spend a week at our desks. Something more active was required. After all, what can one achieve in a week? Simply, I thought, to get one's students to see the *point* of social analysis, to ask new questions and to find out something for themselves.

It is always fascinating to discover how what to the tutor appears to be a very simple question appears as problematical to the student. 'Here we are in a village (I said): who runs it?' A straightforward sociological question: but underneath the question, problems of theory – 'what do we mean by "running" it?' – and problems of method – 'does anybody actually run it and, if so, how do you find out?' Faced with the question, their reaction was: 'What do you mean: who *runs* it?' Exactly: they were already probing beneath the surface of social theory.

'Well,' said I, 'who for example is responsible for deciding that that new school should be built? And who puts the seats on the village green? And who looks after the dustbins? And how is it all paid for?' So, after spending the first hour discussing the matter, we split up into groups which then went off into the village, each with a set of questions to answer. I remember that lunchtime very clearly indeed. For they returned absolutely bursting with excitement. They had actually been talking to some purpose, and they had come into contact with what they called 'real people'. 'And listen,' they said, 'to what we've found out . . .!' And out it all came – among it the fact that the police sergeant's wife had told them that her husband was on duty at the Carlisle assizes and could we go? With the result that half the school went that afternoon at *their* initiative off to the assize courts.

But a head of excitement stimulated by interviewing people is only the beginning of education. For it also needs to be intellectually directed and controlled. Accordingly, notes were made under careful supervision. These were used in writing up a draft account of what had been found out, which, after criticism and discussion, was rewritten by the students to produce a final report on the government of a Cumberland village. 'But how *do* you write it up?' they said, when they brought all their notes together half-way through the course. So it became necessary to explain how to write and how to organise material into a coherent report. And, of course, in the by-going, we had to consider – for how else could we understand what had been found out? – the political and social theory that underpinned the division of power, for example, between the different levels of public authority or between democratic representation and the control of the public purse strings, or which explained why the 'grass-roots' theory of democracy – that the parish council could govern everything – was not viable. Thus, in *doing* the job it became essential to look *beneath* the facts that we had collected in order to consider the political theory which gave the facts their meaning. It thus became necessary for me, as the tutor, to add my specific contribution to a common task, if the job were to be effectively carried out.

Now this is not particularly new. But it set me off on a way of thinking about adult education that I have been developing since then in several other projects. The most advanced procedure is in the work of the Chilterns Society who have carried out a survey of some 3,000 interviews over an area of some 400 square miles in the South Buckinghamshire region, the results of which are now being processed on a computer. But I wish to describe two smaller projects of a simpler kind which have been done in Basingstoke and Maidstone.

Basingstoke is an old market town on the North Hampshire Downs. In 1961 it became involved in a town-development scheme under which its population was to grow from 26,000 to 80,000. When this was made public, the Workers Educational Association began to ask itself whether it could make any contribution to this development scheme, and its chairman came to see me at the University. Don't come to lecture us, he said in effect: help us to find something out! I flung my academic hat in the air for joy at such an approach. Thus developed the idea that we might carry out some research and write a report which could be put into circulation in the borough in order to help people understand what the social problems – and the possibilities – of a town-development scheme might be. Again, the idea of making knowledge for some relevant social purpose.

The project took three years to complete; and it was understood that anyone who enrolled in the group should actually be willing to work on the enquiry. As a result of this, most people were scared off and we began with five members in the class in the first year, though the numbers subsequently grew till we had a group of over a dozen. We got to grips with the issues involved, first of all by making an enquiry among the people who had already moved into Basingstoke to find out why they had moved to the town and how they had settled down, once there. We designed the questionnaire together and rallied a party of university students to help with interviewing over 200 people.

Interviewing is simply a way of making one's own documents. The historian has *his* documents in the library; but the sociologist must often, so to speak, make his own. But then, like the historian, the sociologist has to decide upon the relevance of the information he collects and then analyse it so as to find valid answers to the questions which he is interested in. Once the interviewing was completed, therefore, the group turned to the spadework of classifying the information, analysing it statistically and, finally, of helping to draft an account of what had been found out. In this way, the group itself did some of the cutting and stitching of sociological inquiry and learned from their *own* direct experience what counted intellectually as good and bad stitching: when statistical evidence, for example, was sufficient to support a particular conclusion; when a judiciously chosen quotation would enliven the bare bones of a statistical analysis.

In the second year, we sought to broaden our understanding of the social problems of new communities by reading and annotating a large number of photocopied articles about other towns' experiences which were provided by the Ministry of Housing library in London and the County Library Service. The final year was spent discussing what we should recommend to be *done* in Basingstoke and in drafting the final report.

What we were doing here, in effect, was to turn *adult* education to use in the wider process of *public education*. But we did this in many other ways as well. For in the second session we arranged several visits to other new towns where, with the help of the W.E.A. branch and the local authority, we were shown round and afterwards met for discussion groups of local people who had been active in the life of the town. This was taken a stage further by an architect member of the group who organised a week's tour of the new towns around London, which provided material for a two-page article in the local weekly newspaper and a memorable film, which showed what we had seen and sought to point up its implications for the future development of Basingstoke itself.

It was this work which really shifted my thinking about the role of investigation in adult education. For while the project had given the Basingstoke group a direct experience of actually making knowledge, which had taught them a great deal about the problems that were involved in this process, it had not been as successful as I would have liked. The reason for this was that I had not made it sufficiently clear *from the start* that the group would be responsible for writing its own report; and the reason for that was that it was only as the work developed that I came to see that the critical difference between the ordinary tutorial and an Extra-Mural class regarded as a research-group was that, in the latter case, it was the students themselves and not the tutor who had to accept responsibility for the investigation and for report writing, under the tutor's general guidance and with his full support.

This principle was firmly written into the next, and much more successful project. In 1964, a Council of Churches had been set up in Maidstone. This Council began its deliberations by asking itself what *it* could contribute to the social welfare of the borough. Clearly, the first thing to do was to find out what was going on in the town by way of social welfare provision, so as to be able to answer the question: were there any *gaps* in the service which might be filled either by the Church or by some other agency?

At a large public meeting held under the chairmanship of the vicar of Maidstone, a steering committee was set up for the project. In the event, however, this dwindled in importance and the work was done by a group of about a dozen people. This group met in the vicarage to discuss the project and I eventually joined them in order to thrash out how best to achieve what they had in mind. And here, to the layman's amazement, I began by asking the question: what do you hope to have achieved by producing this report? For that question would govern the purpose of the project and that, in turn, would directly affect how I would advise them to go about doing it. In this case, the group were thinking of interviewing a random sample of ordinary townsfolk; but it was easy to show that, for their particular purpose, it would be much more useful to interview the leading officials – about eighty in all – of all the statutory and voluntary social agencies.

Interviewing of this kind involves both social and what one might call 'forensic' skills: the ability to win and maintain rapport with an informant *and* the ability to cross-examine him so as to get reliable and relevant information. Most of our group – probation officers, personnel managers and the like – had had experience of interviewing in their jobs; but they all went through an intensive weekend training session on interview techniques for research purposes. After a few months' work, they had amassed a great pile of interview notes, which then had to be analysed and sifted and written up in a form that would be suitable for publication.

These two studies are characteristic of a new style of adult education which seems to be growing up. I have myself been involved in two comparable projects in recent years and the work of Coates and Silburn in Nottingham which was shown in our programme 8 of *Teaching Adults* is very similar in method since it was conceived as a way of getting Extra-Mural students to find out knowledge for themselves by engaging directly in investigation. The Nottingham study, however, was primarily intended as an exercise in sociology, whereas the studies that I have described were intended primarily to develop a community's *own* self-awareness and, as such, they have had the following characteristics:

1. They are promoted by the experience of and reaction to social change: in Basingstoke, the question of what social consequences follow from setting up a town-development scheme, which we can seek to adapt to; in Maidstone, how can we, a Council of Churches, define for ourselves a role in the welfare state ?

2. These questions are raised, in the first instance, by a voluntary body like the W.E.A.

3. This organisation then seeks academic support, usually through an Extra-Mural department, which provides it with guidance in methods of enquiry and perhaps a broader theoretical grasp than would otherwise be found, but without usurping the responsibility

of the voluntary agency itself to draft its report and to decide upon matters of policy.

4. The outcome is the preparation of a report by adult-educational methods which is then channelled into the community itself as a means of wider, public education.

This kind of educational activity, involving first-hand social investigation by a local group, the careful analysis and assessment of local circumstances and the preparation of reports, is a fairly recent development, and its main instrument is the social survey. It has the great benefit that it makes it possible for adult education to be active and entertaining, and not just passive. For it *is* great fun to indulge in the legitimized impertinence of knocking on other people's doors and asking questions and collecting facts.

But there are two 'buts'. The first is this. Doing surveys takes a lot of time, manpower and effort which ought not to be used uneconomically. If you want to find out about the difficulties of life in tall blocks of flats, for instance, it may well be easier and more rewarding to read the reports of other people's inquiries first. Never do a survey if you can get the information you want some other way. For the excitement of knocking on doors is preceded by a much longer period of thinking and preparation and a still longer and much more difficult one of analysing and writing up the material.

Secondly, facts are not enough. You also need to have a very clear idea of why, and for what purposes, these *particular* facts are going to be worth collecting. Collecting facts – doing a survey – therefore, is no substitute for thinking. Nor will the facts themselves tell you what you *ought* to do by way of policy or how to go about doing it. If they cannot be a substitute for thinking, neither can they be a substitute for the creative imagination that thinks up new ideas for doing things.

For these reasons, theory is essential to a soundly-framed inquiry; and that is one of the things which a tutor must bring to work of this kind. It is also essential to sound education. Much educational method is based upon the idea that there is a *subject* to be taught and the tutor's job is to teach it. At its best, the tutor is able to catch his students' imagination and to involve them, making contributions out of their own experience, in discussion. At its worst, it produces a situation in which the subject is conceived as a great heap of information which the tutor has to shovel, so to speak, in the form of lectures, into the bucket-minds of his students. It sometimes results in a relationship between tutor and students in which the students sit passively before his authoritative command of the subject and in which, therefore, written work is mere précis of existing knowledge, done under the constraint of the student's doubts about what *he* can possibly say that is new.

The basic idea of these other projects is rather that there is an *argument* to be constructed and that the argument is made by the combined efforts of the students and the tutor. They become collaborators in a common enterprise. For what a sociologist is really doing, in his professional activity, is making arguments: not arguments in the sense that the layman uses the term, as equivalent to 'quarrels', but arguments as the product of sound factual information, tightly sewn together to *say* something: something that will be intellectually sound and practically useful in helping us to look at things more clearly and correctly. By trying to make good arguments, we learn something about the intellectual *discipline* that is involved – that is to say, about the kind of theory that is involved and the methods for establishing it – and that, after all, is the nub of sociology or any other academic study.

This kind of idea, and the teaching by investigation that grows out of it, is applicable to other studies as well as to sociology. It is already used in geographical field-studies, in archaeology and in that fascinating new area of investigation, industrial archaeology. And it can be usefully extended to many other fields.

In social history, for example, a useful project could be developed around the question (of intrinsic interest to a Manchester man with a Liverpool suit!) of the origins and validity of the distinction between 'Manchester man, Liverpool gentleman'. What was the difference between the social groups that influenced the growth of these two cities? Who *were* the people, for example, who established their two great orchestras and can anything be learned about them by finding out, for instance, why the one is the plain Hallé, while the other – in the city of gentlemen – is now the *Royal* Liverpool Philharmonic?

Such a problem would require the students not simply to sit and listen to the tutor but actually to go to the documents themselves – in the city libraries or in the archives of the orchestras – to sift and sort the evidence and to compare critically *for themselves* data which, under a tutor's guidance – under two tutors even, if two study-groups in two cities could collaborate in the matter – could probably be shown to be relevant for a wider understanding of the nineteenth-century city.

In such projects the role of the tutor is still critical: but rather as a science tutor might set up the apparatus for an experiment that the students would do, than as an authoritative dominie. He also has a crucial role in making use of his broader grasp of a discipline to point up the significance of, and the problems that are involved in the detailed enquiries which his students would be carrying out. This can be seen very clearly in the film of the Nottingham project. For that investigation illustrates very clearly the crucial point that to involve people in actually making knowledge – to teach by investigation – is the best way to get them to understand *from inside* what knowledge is all about.

Further reading

BROADY, M. *Planning for people* National Council of Social Service, 1969.

BROADY, M. The Maidstone project in *Social Service Quarterly* Spring 1966.

COATES, K. and SILBURN, R. *Poverty, deprivation and morale in a Nottingham community* Nottingham University, 1967.

MOSER, C. A. *Survey methods in social investigation* Heinemann, 1958.

WARREN, R. *Studying your community* New York: Free P., 1965; Collier-Macmillan, 1965.

MAIDSTONE COUNCIL OF CHURCHES. *Maidstone: a closer look*, 1965.

WORKERS EDUCATIONAL ASSOCIATION, SOUTHERN DISTRICT. *Basingstoke: a social survey*, 1966.

WHAT IS THE POINT OF ADULT EDUCATION?

by Roy Shaw

Everyone acknowledges the noble past of adult education, but what should be its main concerns now, and what is its relevance to the present day? What is its future? How much difference will the Open University make? Should we increasingly encourage external standards of assessment? Professor Roy Shaw, Director of the Department of Adult Education at the University of Keele, gives here a personal view of some of the challenges and contemporary difficulties of the adult education world.

It may seem odd to ask the question asked in the title of this chapter. After all adult education exists, in all its diversity, so isn't the question rather like that of the little girl who asked at a party: 'Mummy, what is that man for?' However, adult education is an activity involving organisation and teaching strategies, and both depend on convictions about the purpose, or purposes, of adult education. For example, the W.E.A. was brought into being because of the very definite convictions of Albert Mansbridge and others that something special should be done to promote the higher education of working men and women. Those who work in adult education now may not be conscious of any need to ask questions about the point of adult education – like the man the little girl asked about, it is just there. But asking questions may help to clarify purposes and assumptions by making them explicit. These assumptions, though they may be unacknowledged, sometimes unconscious, sometimes even conflicting, shape our activity, whether we know it or not.

The first of many points about adult education is that it is based on the assumption that education is not simply something which is done to children, but is an activity which should go on throughout life. We may distinguish between learning from experience, self-education and organised education. In a sense, we have always realised that education is life-long. We say 'You live and learn', and use grandiose phrases like 'the University of life'. In America, credit is given in external degree courses for 'life experience', and it is right that it should. Life experience is part of any adult's equipment. It is not the same as self-education which implies a more deliberate attempt at learning. The public library is perhaps one of the main aids to self-education, but nowadays books are supplemented by radio and television programmes. The value of self-education was emphasised in Gibbon's famous remark that every man has two educations, one that is given to him, another much more valuable that he gets for himself. In the past, 'given' education was confined to youth, and self-education was the activity of maturity. There have always been a few brave spirits who have achieved wonders by self-education, but for the majority it is a path that is very difficult to follow, requiring heroic self-discipline to persist. Many would-be self-educators fall by the wayside. Hence the value of organised adult education, which offers the adult student the stimulus of a teacher and fellow-students. It is coming to be recognised that provision of adult education is as important as that for children and young people.

Sometimes the phrase 'life-long education' is used. Education should certainly go on throughout life, but although I have a vested interest in providing organised adult education, I don't believe that adults must attend adult education courses throughout life. It is true that in what is sometimes called the adult education movement, especially in the W.E.A., a minority do become life-long course attenders, covering the whole range of subjects, from philosophy to Persian art, from economics to modern drama. Some programming encourages this life-long addiction to class attendance. It is certainly convenient for organisers to have the same people enrolling year after year, but it is questionable whether it is the best use of limited resources. Adult education always caters for a minority of the population, but it should be a constantly changing minority. The aim of adult education should be self-education, and one would normally expect that having acquired a skill in a course or having been grounded in a body of knowledge, the adult student would be able to carry on under his own steam, with perhaps the occasional refresher course.

Adult education has always been associated with the idea of a democratic society. Some of it seems to be based on what might be called 'the fallacy of the omniscient citizen': the belief that all adult citizens can learn all there is to know by constant course attendance, or worse still, by attending regular single lectures or conferences on every subject under the sun. Such a promiscuous desire to know is self-frustrating and can lead to widespread half-knowledge that is worse than plain ignorance. Pope's famous warning is perhaps not sufficiently heeded in adult education:

> A little learning is a dang'rous Thing;
> Drink deep, or taste not the Pierian Spring:
> There shallow Draughts intoxicate the Brain,
> And drinking largely sobers us again.

It is often objected that most people do not have the time (or the capacity?) to drink deeply, and don't they have the right to dabble in knowledge if they wish? The right is certainly there, but it does not follow that it is a proper use of adult education facilities to cater for it, particularly when it is increasingly catered for by the mass media. The newspapers (especially the colour supplements), radio and television programmes are full of material which caters for this need. At least since the magazine *Titbits* was founded in the late nineteenth century, it has been a profitable business to feed the public mind with gobbets of information. In my view this activity does not so much educate as *opinionate*, giving people superficial opinions on a vast range of subjects, because it is assumed that all must be equipped with such opinions. There was more wisdom in the adult educator who said that the art of life consists in the selection of one's ignorances.

If adult education is not going to be a dispenser of 'shallow draughts' of knowledge, what is it for? I doubt whether it is really possible to find a single purpose which will embrace all forms of adult education, from the army mechanics' training course to a tutorial class in philosophy, from the archaeological dig to the practical Yoga group. If there is such a single point, it will have to be very general. 'Self-improvement' perhaps? This could certainly cover the improvement of practical skills, the development of a body of knowledge, the conservation of health and the pursuit of wisdom. Like all statements about education, 'self-improvement' implies a value judgment: it is better to be skilled, physically fit and knowledgeable than to be unskilled, unfit, and ignorant. This may seem too obvious, but it needs to be said in view of the fashionable scepticism about educational and cultural values. Jeremy Bentham started the trouble when he said that 'Quantity of pleasure being equal pushpin is as good as poetry'. (Pushpin was a trivial game played with pins. The modern equivalent might be shove ha'penny.) If an adult finds a greater quantity of pleasure in the pub than in the evening class, it is difficult to persuade him that 'it is better for him' to turn to adult education. We have even invented the term 'do-gooder' to discredit anyone who tries to help people to better themselves.

But in the English adult education tradition mere self-improvement has sometimes been frowned upon as egotistical. Great emphasis used to be placed on the social purpose of learning – using learning to improve social conditions, or to serve the community, as a local councillor for example. At its best, this was an admirable tradition; at its worst, it degenerated into philistinism, dismissing subjects like music and literature as 'dilettante' (a very dirty word when I became a tutor), while worth-while study was confined to subjects like economics and industrial relations. Now the pendulum has swung to the other extreme, and it may be timely to utter warnings that learning *can* become a form of spiritual avarice, though this applies to all learning and does not imply acceptance of the view that the arts are the opium of the intellectuals. On the other hand, there is a new philistinism which takes the form of regarding non-vocational studies as expendable luxuries, forgetting that living means more than livelihood. So it is still important to preserve a balance between a narrow utilitarianism and a selfish dilettantism in approaching adult education.

We need to know what adult education is for if only to know how to commend it to those for whom it is intended. Adults may need education, but the need is not always felt. Children may still sullenly learn subjects even though they see 'no point in them'; undergraduates are beginning to rebel, and adults are under no compulsion to study unless they want to. So there is usually a question in a potential student's mind: 'What is the point of my studying this subject?' – something which those who live with the subject too often forget, since the question was settled to their satisfaction years ago. How, then, do you get people to sample adult education? Some sceptics come to their first adult class for purely accidental reasons (I went to my first to be with a girl friend). Once there, they may stay; but how do you get them to take the first step? Not, as a rule, by theoretical argument. You may tell people that Guinness is good for them or that Mackeson does them good, but such arguments for educational offerings will be counter-productive, although they are true. Of course, the drinks and the pubs you drink them in have been promoted by millions of pounds' worth of ingenious advertising. They are presented as enjoyable, voluntary adult activities (people under 18 not eligible); whereas education by comparison is miserably promoted, and is associated in most adult minds with compulsory attendance at (often) dismal premises for dosing with unappetising medicine.

So, adult educators, who mostly do not have captive audiences, have a difficult task in attracting and holding their students. 'Will there be an adequate recruitment?' and 'Will they stay now they've come?' are the anxious questions which haunt most organisers and teachers in adult education. They suffer from a further handicap. As honest men they cannot offer the instant wisdom and 'rapid results' which many commercial providers of education and training facilities promise. One of the points of adult education is that it involves effort. The best teacher of adults can only help those who help themselves. He can no more 'give' you skill and understanding than a physical culturist can 'give' fitness or muscular development. Nevertheless, I have listened to many teaching sessions where this fact is ignored. Too many teachers act on a tacit assumption that they *can* give their student understanding or wisdom. They tell all, and little of it is assimilated. The rule that students should not be taught more than they can learn is regularly broken. Dr Belbin quotes a Chinese proverb, 'We learn something from what we hear, more from what we see, and most from what we do.' There is another which says, 'What I hear I forget, what I do I know.' This principle is illustrated by one of my own adult students, a grocer's wife, who was assuring a new recruit of the value of doing written work. 'You learn more by doing the essays than you do by coming to the lectures,' she said – and I know this was a testimony to the value of personal activity in education rather than a criticism of the lectures.

So it seems that self-education remains the core of adult education, but organised courses may encourage self-education, providing guidance and discipline. One difficulty in achieving the proper degree of student effort is that most adult education attendance is still voluntary. The pattern is changing, as the amount of day-release and full-time training grows. In such courses it is easier to require student effort. In voluntary courses the teacher has to evoke it. This requires considerable teaching skill, and one which success in school or university teaching does not necessarily guarantee. Hence, part-time tutors (as well as voluntary students) often find the requirement of student effort in what is sometimes called 'liberal' education (the word will be discussed below) a great bugbear. It is accepted as inevitable in practical courses like joinery or dressmaking, but not in literature or history. 'They are happy enough to come to lectures,' I have heard teachers say very often, 'but they won't do written work.' One is reminded of the dictum that there are no bad students, only bad teachers; far too often student reluctance to be involved in personal effort is a reflection of the tutor's approach. As I mentioned above, he may often plan his course on the assumption that it is his job to tell the students all they need to know, rather than to get them to find out for themselves. Hence the request for any form of student effort (essays, maps, surveys – even discussion) seems like an unpleasant penance inflicted on students to satisfy bureaucratic requirements, rather than an integral part of the course. When this happens it is my experience that the whole teaching approach, from the syllabus construction onwards, has been misconceived, and the fault will not be remedied by even the most tactful and persuasive pleas for students' work. What I am saying is that many teachers miss the point of adult education. They see themselves as founts of wisdom, spraying the surrounding students with the waters of learning which the students need only soak up. In fact, most of it runs like water off a duck's back, and I am sadly convinced that countless teaching hours are wasted every year (and not only in adult education, of course) by teachers deluging their hearers with material that is very largely forgotten. It is perhaps relevant to recall that one of television's most beguiling presenters of 'serious' programmes, Mr Malcolm Muggeridge, has confessed that although everyone knows him as a television personality, he has never met anyone who remembers anything he has said on television. He doubtless exaggerates, but there is a caution in his tale.

It has been said that the whole institution of lecturing ignores the invention of the printed book. It is true that many lecturers do present an oral version of what would be better read. Still, lecturing has a point. Its job is to stimulate, to make connections and to provoke critical examination of what has been read. There used to be a tradition in adult education classes that a two-hour session should consist of one hour's lecture, one hour's discussion. This pattern still survives in many classes, although many of us have learnt from experience (supported by research evidence) that an hour is far too long for uninterrupted talking. Most people's capacity to attend and absorb is exhausted long before, and it is more effective if the lecturing part of the class is broken into several short stints. Even then, the best lecture to a class (unlike a public lecture to an audience) should be a teaching lecture rather than an oration. That is, it should be so framed as to solicit participation in the form of questions or comment. I know from visiting courses that far too many lecturers go on relentlessly for even more than an hour, and that the so-called 'discussion' period very often consists of brief questions from a few of the braver spirits in the class which elicit a series of lengthy lecturettes from the lecturer.

The foregoing could be summed up by saying that the point of adult education is what the student himself does, and what the teacher does should be to inspire and guide student effort. The danger of some approaches to teacher training is that they encourage concentration on the teacher's performance as a thing in itself, whereas it should always be seen in the context of the teaching relationship. The growth of one-way means of teaching (radio, television) encourages those in live adult education to emphasise the problem of feedback, and to contrast the passive listener or viewer with the lively exchange of the class situation. This is a loaded comparison, taking television at its worst, and live adult education at its best. Mr Joseph Weltman, when he was Education Officer for the Independent Television Authority, rightly challenged the tendency of adult educators to compare an *ideal* of live adult education with the *reality* of broadcast adult education. He admits that although broadcast adult education is supposed, according to a Government formula to lead 'to progressive mastery of a skill or a body of knowledge', there is little evidence that this is achieved, but he questions whether education on television is in this respect very different from a great many traditional liberal education or general cultural courses conducted by, for example, the W.E.A. or University Extra-Mural departments. 'Tutors and lecturers are satisfied,' he says, 'if sufficient students enrol for their courses; they congratulate themselves if a large enough portion persist to the end of the course. Subjective impressions of academic achievement are impressive, but scarcely conclusive.'

On the other hand, Mr Weltman, like some others in broadcasting, underestimates the importance of what the student does for himself when he claims that broadcast adult education is at least as successful as live adult education in reaching 'those very large numbers of people who are ready to receive cultural enlightenment, but are either unwilling or unable to seek it through the discipline of officially organised class or group work'. That phrase 'receive cultural enlightenment', begs most of the questions argued above. Enlightenment has to be worked for not merely received. It is precisely the weaker brethren who will be most helped by the supportive atmosphere of the 'officially organised class or group'. This is not to deny that broadcasts, supported by publications, cannot be cunningly planned to induce self-help, but it is not surprising that they fail to do this even more often than live teachers.

The difficulty of inducing student effort springs in part from the voluntary attendance which characterises most adult education, and the absence of examinations and similar inducements to effort. Traditionally, adult education has been haunted by a belief that diplomas and certificates (and the examinations they involve) are somehow foreign to its spirit. I have often heard them peremptorily dismissed as 'bits of paper' that no self-respecting student should want. Quite recently, I have heard a tutor advance the view that if there must be examinations in adult education, then they should be examinations where everyone passes. Nevertheless, there is now a growing number of diploma and certificate courses involving examination, run by university Extra-Mural departments, notably London. It might seem ironical that examinations are gaining ground in adult education at a time when their value is being seriously questioned in, for example, university undergraduate education. But there are experiments in the kind of examination – such as allowing students to take in books – and there are moves to introduce continuous assessment either as a supplement to examinations or as a replacement for them.

But any form of assessment puts more responsibility on teachers and taught to measure up to objective standards of achievement, and both have a growing place in adult education. The old arguments about 'knowledge for its own sake' have a fine ring about them, and certainly at its very best this tradition achieved and still achieves remarkable results. Often however it is a rationalisation of a distaste for objective measures of achievement.

In adult education at its worst, it is even easier to 'get away with murder' than it is in other forms of education – which is saying a lot. It is not only the students who must exercise great self-discipline in adult education. Its general freedom from external evaluation calls for great integrity in the teacher. Happily, this integrity is widespread, particularly among full-time teachers in adult education. It is fostered by professional tradition, and to some extent encouraged by inspection and regulations. I say to some extent, because inspection calls for

Solomon standards of wisdom in the inspectors, and no visitor on a single visit to a course sees the course as it really is. As for regulations, they are a necessary evil. Necessary, because they suggest minimum standards of achievement; evil because they encourage mechanical observance and encourage the belief that, for example, students must do 'written work' to 'satisfy the regulations', when the real reason for doing it is to satisfy the demands of the subject, and indeed to satisfy students themselves.

Associated with the growth of examinations and qualifications in adult education is the development of vocational or semi-vocational adult education, ranging from workshop training to full-time courses for probation officers and child care officers. This growth is also seen by some as inimical to the true spirit of adult education. Many years ago, Professor R. H. Tawney, a great prophet of adult education, epigrammatically said that the point of adult education was not to help you to get on in life, but to help the life get on in you. It is a remark which I repeated many times with approval, while my experience was limited to non-vocational adult education. Later, however, I learnt from experience that it is possible to teach people on a vocational course in a liberal manner. (It is also possible to teach a non-vocational course in an illiberal manner.) Just what do we mean by 'liberal'? We know that historically it derives from classical times, indicating the education given to a free man as opposed to that given to a slave. Those who still look down on vocational courses are perhaps implicitly looking on work as slavery, or at any rate as the unfree part of a man's life. Real life, it is assumed, begins only in leisure. This view is as one-sided and wrong-headed as the one at the opposite extreme which thinks that vocational training alone is important. Work is a central part of living, and education for life should include education for work. A vocation is a noble and not a mean thing, and many people (social workers, for example) are dedicated to their work. It is true that vocational education is still too often narrowly conceived in terms of training in particular skills or vocational subjects – like economics for the trade unionist or social psychology for the social worker. The point of adult education is that the adult student needs self-knowledge if he is to do his job well, and this means that subjects like individual psychology or English literature are highly relevant. This is by no means generally acknowledged, particularly in industry where talk of 'management skills' encourages the notion that handling people is very much like handling machinery. This mechanical approach will not only fail with other people but it is often harmful to the individual himself. An American poet warned an audience of business executives that 'an ulcer is an unkissed imagination taking its revenge for having been jilted. It is an unwritten poem, neglected music, an unpainted watercolour, an undanced dance'. In other words vocational education must develop the student as a person and not simply as an executive or an operative. The growth of work sponsored by Industrial Training Boards makes realisation of this fact more urgent. Businessmen often take short views and see value only in training for functions as distinct from the education of the man, whereas the two cannot really be separated. There are signs that some I.T.B.'s are inclined to look favourably on broadly based educational programmes, and all who care for the health of industry will want to see this tendency grow. It would involve a recognition that workpeople are no longer to be thought of merely as 'hands' but as human beings with heads and hearts as well. For better and worse, the whole man is involved in industry.

A danger in vocational courses involving examination and qualifications is, of course, that the qualification becomes an end in itself, but it need not do so. Universities have for centuries more or less successfully combined liberal education and training for the professions of law and medicine for example. The exam fetish is a perversion of the exam system and it is worth pointing out that education-without-exams or qualifications has its own perversions. Where there is no objective discipline students may work or not as they choose and if unwanted pressure is put on them, they may (in most adult education) leave the course. Faced with this situation, the teacher has two alternatives before him. He may achieve the difficult task (discussed above) of inducing the student to impose self-discipline; or he may soft-pedal the demands of study and pander to his students to keep the course going. This temptation is particularly strong for a part-time teacher whose fee depends on the continuance of the course. Again, this need not happen, and when it does it is a perversion of adult-education-without-exams.

So far, this chapter has largely concentrated on courses involving sustained study by the participants, not only or mainly in the form of essays but also in the form of notes, diagrams, maps, lecturettes, surveys, models, etc. There are at least two kinds of course where these are not appropriate: very elementary ones and advanced ones. As for elementary courses, I have already indicated scepticism about the value of short courses on big subjects at an elementary level. Some have helped to give 'liberal studies' a bad name. It is too often assumed that technical subjects must be done thoroughly and at length, but 'liberal' subjects can be dealt with briefly and superficially. I have been approached by a head of a liberal studies department of a college for advice on a scheme to give his students a liberal education by bringing in a philosopher one week to 'tell them about philosophy', and a historian the next to do the same for his subject, and so on. Worse still, I have heard of a candidate for a liberal studies teaching post who proposed to do a course on psychoanalysis who, when asked why and whether he had made a study of it, replied: 'No, but I've had it.' I hasten to say that there is, of course, a great deal of very exciting work being done in liberal studies up and down the country – but perhaps not enough. A remarkable example of how demanding creative and liberating liberal studies can be is to be found in the justly famous work of Mr Albert Hunt at the Bradford College of Art.

There is obviously scope for elementary courses on recreational and practical subjects like Flower Arrangement, Cookery and Car Maintenance, particularly as these involve student participation all the way. It is more difficult to see the justification for short elementary courses on subjects like Art History, Commerce, Religion or Psychology – unless these are planned as 'trailers' for a longer course. The only people who can really benefit from short courses in such subjects are those who already have a good grounding in them and want to take them further to be brought up to date. It is obviously absurd to apply the same pattern of course length and student participation to a group of graduate economists working as executives in industry, as to a group of miners beginning to study Economics. Even in advanced courses, however, there should be plenty of scope for participation. (I have been at too many conferences to be very impressed by the value of simply listening to talks, however brilliant they may be.)

Given the availability of higher education in the past few decades one would expect a demand for advanced levels of adult education gradually to increase. And it has. Both post-graduate and updating courses are becoming common in adult education, and in the last few years there has been increasing pressure not only for certificates and diplomas, but also for external degrees. The main available source of external degrees in this country – the University of London – has been overwhelmed by the number of would-be students, although many people feel that the London curriculum is far from suitable to the needs of adult students. It is to meet the need of adult students who want to take degrees externally that the Open University has been established. It offers degrees which can be gained by part-time study for 'credits' over a period of years, using a sophisticated teaching system combining radio, television, recordings, books, correspondence courses and live teaching. Some have seen in the establishment of the Open University a threat to adult education. I can see only a challenge to established methods of teaching and a completion of the adult education system by meeting the ever-growing demand for part-time study at degree level. There seems to be good reason to expect large numbers of students to be forthcoming.

But however many Open University students there are, they will still represent only the narrowing top section of the adult education pyramid. The broad base will continue for decades to be the vast majority of the population who lack even secondary education, let alone a degree. Many more than we perhaps imagine are capable of study at degree level but not even utopian educationists can ignore the fact that most people will not have the ability or the desire to work at this level, but they still have needs for adult education which should be met. It is in dealing with the broad masses of people that adult education strategy needs to be re-thought. The point of W.E.A.–University Extra-Mural work was once conceived as catering for the higher education of 'working men and women'. For many years now this kind of work has followed the example of the Mechanics' Institutes of the nineteenth century by catering increasingly for what R. H. Tawney once called the 'educationally sophisticated' – those people, largely middle class, who already know the value of education and are easily drawn to courses. But the point of adult education has always been that it has a 'missionary' purpose to convert to educational pursuits those whose background had made education distasteful to them and those who have the latent ability rather than the felt desire to study further. I am old enough (and old-fashioned enough) to cherish memories of working with groups of miners, railway workers, agricultural workers and housewives, starting from scratch, and leading them on to sustained study over a period of years. I remember with particular satisfaction a successful course of this kind which not only impressed the visiting inspector by the quality of its work, but inspired him to recall John Wesley's advice to his emissaries: 'Go not to those who need you, but to those who need you most.' There is a danger nowadays that those who need education most, and are therefore the most difficult to bring to it, may be largely left outside adult education provison, though local authority evening institutes do large numbers of practical and hobby courses for them. The adult education audience, sizeable though it is, is still a minority of the population and the vast majority are left to swell the millions whose leisure is dominated by the television. I have heard adult education organisers curse the 'idiot box', but to do this is to overlook the opportunities which television presents. It is true that a good many radio and television programmes are superficial rubbish, but so are a good many printed books – as any railway bookstall should remind us. But a significant proportion of radio and television programming is educative (as distinct from educational) even if at a fairly superficial level. Willy-nilly, broadcasting and the press are part of the country's adult education system, and adult educators should be concerned with what Raymond Williams has called 'the politics of culture', doing what they can individually and through organisations to improve the general educative role of broadcasting, and where possible developing joint work with broadcasting agencies in specifically educational courses. So far, broadcast adult education has not had anything like the impact of which it is capable, and it is striking that the most profound influence of broadcasting on adult education has not been by educational programmes but by general programmes such as the archaeological quiz programmes which are generally credited with stimulating the growth of archaeology in adult education. Sir Kenneth Clark's 'Civilisation' series may have a similar effect.

Education as a whole has still to take the measure of television not only as a cultural influence but also as a subject for study itself. There are technical difficulties in studying television which may shortly be relieved by the development of convenient and inexpensive recording systems for vision as well as sound. Then we might begin to see a proper acknowledgement of the role of television in contemporary life. For example, it would be more fruitful to study television drama with a group of apprentices or working-class wives, than to begin with Greek drama or Shakespeare. In the vast output of television drama inevitably much is inferior, but so is most of the output of the live theatre. There is a significant proportion of good television drama and it speaks to the experience of the vast majority of the population much more directly than (say) Shakespeare.

Television and journalism are often dismissed by educationists as mere 'popularisation'; but popularisation means simply making popular what is good. In Matthew Arnold's phrase, it means making the best of culture available outside the clique of the cultivated and learned. Mr Kenneth Allsop has said that he sees his job as a television interviewer as asking 'pertinent questions on behalf of fellow laymen, and drawing replies from experts in a language that is intelligible to people at large'. Mr Cliff Michelmore has said of his role as a broadcaster, 'what pleases me is to simplify complex problems'. Any adult educator who has struggled to simplify complex problems knows the challenge, and the satisfaction of meeting it. Of course, there is always the danger of over-simplification, and not everything can be made simple, but if democratic education means anything, it means that some people must work hard to divest learning of unnecessary difficulty, and to make as much as possible 'understanded of the people'.

It could be said that popularisation is *the* point of most adult education – assuming that 'education for the educated', important as it is, will for a long time remain a subsidiary aspect. Popularisation at its best springs from a 'missionary' impulse which has always been found in English adult education. The term can sound offensively religiose, or suggest patronising expeditions to those that dwell in the darkness of ignorance; but we should remember that adult education owes part of its motive force in the past to specifically Christian inspiration. That has largely gone, but we cannot afford to lose the moral inspiration that leads some scholars to want to share their scholarship or their skills with as many people as possible – in the literal sense of the word, to *broadcast* them. This impulse is simply the expression of charity, of justice, in the sphere of learning. Man does not live by fair shares of bread alone.

The point of adult education is an expression of the point of Christianity, of humanism, and of democracy. It is that men should have life more abundantly, should cultivate their human qualities and should play a responsible role in society.

Further reading

RECONSTRUCTION, Ministry of, Adult Education Committee *A design for democracy*; with an introd. 'The years between' by R. D. Waller. Parrish, 1956.
MACLEAN, R. *Television in education* Methuen, 1968.
SCUPHAM, J. *Broadcasting and the community* Watts, 1967.
HUNT, A. The Bradford bolsheviks in *New Society* 23 Nov. 1967, p. 733.

THE ORGANISERS
by William Carter

What can the organiser-principal or L.E.A. adviser do for the individual teacher? How can close contacts be developed between the Institute and the community around it? William Carter, Further Education Adviser for the City of Sheffield, suggests some of the answers in this chapter.

Who *are* the organisers? In England and Wales the local education authorities, the university Extra-Mural departments and the Workers' Educational Association together employ about 150 administrators in adult education and about 1,500 principals and organisers. Some of the administrators, particularly those employed by local authorities, also have duties in other branches of education. Most of the principals and organisers, however, work wholly in the field of adult education. Some look after areas and regions, others work in local branches, centres or institutes.

I want to discuss the role of the local education authority organiser and, in particular, the relationship between the work that he does in his centre or in his area and the work of the teacher and the adult student.

This relationship needs to be a very close one. Yet there are occasions when an organiser is only too well aware that his role is misunderstood. For example, when he meets a teacher whose first response is to produce the attendance register, as though all he expects is an on-the-spot calculation as to whether or not his class should be allowed to continue; or the student who says, 'Ah! You'll have come because we complained last week about the cold!'

Is it the basic insecurity of the part-time teacher which leads him to think that the regulations are more important than the work he and his class are doing? Is the student's faintly belligerent tone of voice a sign that authority, for him, is remote and bureaucratic? Or is it that the organiser visits the class so infrequently that when he does appear no one quite knows why he has come? The misunderstanding, anyway, is there. He has been placed as the man who prepares the way and makes the paths straight and then, except for the occasional visit, leaves the class to make its journey alone.

Of course, much of an organiser's time is taken up in making preparations: in estimating costs, devising courses, appointing and training teachers, arranging publicity, finding accommodation, framing and interpreting regulations. And it is also his job to deal as efficiently as he can with all the administrative problems which teachers and students bring to him from time to time. He has to do whatever is necessary to bring the teacher and the student usefully together so that the process of education can begin. But he can do none of these things with much success unless he is also pretty deeply involved in what happens next.

Whatever expertise he may have as an administrator will be of little practical use unless it grows out of an intimate and up-to-date knowledge of the problems of teaching and learning in the classroom. The assumptions which were part of his preparation have to be checked: Who are the students? Why are they here? How much do they know? How quickly can they learn? Are the aims of the course as relevant and the methods of the teacher as helpful as he had hoped they would be?

These questions are asked in every branch of education. But they are especially important to the organiser and the teacher in adult education because a good deal of adult education today has to be deliberately designed to find the answers to them.

At one time, most evening institute courses were planned to lead to a qualification – commercial, technical, trade or domestic – and the person who joined them found his education charted for him, designed to take him from one level of competence to another in a particular job or profession. His aim was clear. So was his suitability for a course. When he had qualified, the institute had fulfilled its purpose for him. But most vocational courses are now provided in colleges of further education and the average evening institute or centre for adult education has a different kind of job to do.

There are always courses which can be planned for known or specific groups of people: the training course in a particular job or skill, the language course for the student who has reached a known, measurable standard, or the pre-retirement course for people of 55 or 60. A great deal of information about those who need courses of that kind is readily available and we can use it to design a syllabus which, from the start, is very closely related to their purposes. But many institute courses are not of that kind.

They are courses based on a scheme of work that is adaptable enough to allow for a radical change of pace or a new direction as the aptitudes, abilities, needs and interests of the students become evident. Or, they are courses especially designed to reveal these things to the teacher and to the student: 'taster' courses or 'grouped' courses which give the student a chance to test his interests and skills in various ways before he makes up his mind. For what, after all, do we know about the people who will come to our institutes and centres this year, many of them for the first time?

First, they are adults, and this, in itself, determines the kind of environment and the nature of the relationships we need to establish. But they will be adults whose ages may range from 19 or 20 to 60 or 70, and age conditions the pace at which we learn, our attitudes to learning and often our approach to the whole idea of education. We know that some will have a rich educational background and some will not; that some will join a particular class knowing precisely why and some will be happy to experiment with anything the centre has to offer. We know that a good many will come for reasons which, to start with anyway, have little or nothing to do with education – to keep a friend or a next-door neighbour company, to meet other people, or simply to have a night out. What does this mean for the institute, the organiser and the teacher?

Well, first of all, it doesn't mean responding slavishly to all the changing fashions of popular demand. The courses offered and the way in which they develop will depend on what is educationally worth while. But it does mean that the institute has to respond, in its organisation and its teaching, to the kind of person the student, when he enrols, turns out to be. And then, when he is engaged in the learning process, it has to respond to the changes in him which that process brings about. Organising, then, isn't a job for the organiser alone. He has to do it in co-operation with the teacher, and the student himself.

Some years ago, as the principal of a centre, I felt that some changes were needed in our teaching of art. We ran several classes and, in a conventional way, they were all quite successful. That is, their members attended regularly and, year after year, came back to enrol for the new session. They had mastered a certain range of techniques – in oils, water-colour or gouache – and, on occasions, one or other of them would sell a picture for quite a respectable sum. But few of them appeared to enjoy what they were doing. Their work was certainly competent. But it was dull. The problem was to discover whether, at least in some of them, there were not considerable talents which the classes were failing to draw out and develop. When I discussed this with the teachers, one of them said to me, 'I'm afraid that I've helped to make some of my students complacent!'

We decided that it was time for the centre to offer exhibition space to other artists – the best we could find. Over a year or so, with the help of the regional college of art, we mounted a series of art shows which no one coming to the centre could really ignore. The latest pop painting would confront you as you drank your coffee in the canteen. The most baffling of abstracts was waiting for you round the corner as you went back to your classroom.

Of course, there were some results which we hadn't anticipated: late-night arguments with total strangers about the nature and purpose of art; demands from students of dressmaking, philosophy or drama for a seminar on the modern artist. An embarrassing number of people now wanted to take up sketching and painting for themselves. For the art classes, however, the effect was largely what we had planned for.

Some members adopted a new approach or a development of style which gave their work greater confidence and personal validity. Others began slowly to discover in themselves the need to start painting again from the beginning. And others were confirmed and strengthened in their knowledge that the kind of work they had always done was right for them. Finally, a new kind of class began to emerge from further discussion between students and teachers: a group without a regular teacher, to which professional artists were invited from time to time, simply to bring their work-in-progress, to sit in with the group – and to speak if they were spoken to.

The point of describing this experiment at length is to emphasise the complexity of the relationships which help to make an institute responsive in its teaching and flexible in its organisation. The teacher and the student are each involved, in various ways and at various times, with the organiser, in maintaining the quality and the relevance of what is aimed at and what is done. There is the relationship of the organiser and the teacher, which helps to establish appropriate starting points, environments and stimuli; the relationship of the teacher and the student through which most of the process of education is carried on; and the relationship of the student and the organiser through which the student's involvement in adult education, and his commitment to it, can be enlarged. These are 'team' relationships. But the organiser has an additional responsibility: he has to see that the other members of the team are suitably involved.

The involvement of the teacher is not always easy to achieve. The part-time teacher, after all, has only a part-time commitment. He may come to the institute on two or three evenings a week but, normally, only when he has a class to teach. He will have very little time on those evenings to do more than that. The classroom effectively isolates him from other teachers and other students. If the organiser has something to discuss with him he is likely to feel that he can't bring him out of the classroom to do it; and he might interrupt the class for too long if he goes in. On the other hand, if the teacher expects to find the organiser free to talk to him when the classes are over he will often be disappointed.

That kind of situation increases the new part-timer's sense of isolation. In his more experienced colleagues it encourages a frame of mind in which the details of organisation, especially when they go wrong, can seem to be the only things that really matter. It is bad enough if that special piece of equipment he wanted to use has been left in someone else's classroom, or if the office can't find his class register, or if the caretaker rattles his keys at nine o'clock when another ten minutes of classtime would make all the difference. But it is ten times worse if there is no one to complain to about it. Perhaps only a super-efficient organisation can prevent situations of that kind – some trivial, some comic, some important – from ever occurring.

But an institute needs super efficiency rather less than it needs a sense of community. Naturally, the principal must have expertise in management. The office work should be efficient, the timetabling accurate, the communications effective and the lines of authority clearly established. It is even more important, however, that the teacher, the student, the clerk and the caretaker should share a feeling of responsibility for getting these things right. As a teacher, membership of this community means accepting a place in it which is larger than the commitment you have to your own classes. It means involvement in organising as well as teaching – in mounting exhibitions, planning institute projects and surveys, arranging vacation visits – and doing these things in conjunction with students and other teachers.

Most teachers welcome such opportunities. I have found that they welcome, even more, having regular opportunities for discussing and evaluating the work of their classes with their colleagues and the institute principal or organiser. In fact, there is a case to be made for reducing the length of at least one term in the year so that all the teachers in an institute can be free, for a day or two of meetings, to sit down and talk to each other about their classes, their students and their problems. And teachers from other institutes can usefully be brought in so that a group for each main subject that is taught can come together in this way.

'In-service training' sounds too grand a name to give to a meeting of that kind. But that is what it is. As a piece of training, a relatively informal staff meeting, provided it is held regularly, can sometimes be as valuable as a structured course. And the teacher will certainly feel happier about the idea of being 'trained' if it is clear that the problems that arise from his experience, and his ideas of how to deal with them, are valuable material for general discussion.

In the context of regular dialogue between teachers and organisers, more formal and extended training programmes are, naturally, better supported and the need for them more readily accepted. A good deal of thought is now being given to the training of teachers of adults. Most parts of the country have their own training schemes, co-ordinated in each area by the regional Council for Further Education. The local principal and organiser will want to make sure that when his teachers take part in regional training courses they don't regard them as something exceptional: a once-for-all updating of attitudes and methods. At the same time, he will welcome the opportunity that formal teacher training brings for the sustained study of aims, methods and ideas.

Training run outside the institute, in co-operation with other centres and involving teachers and organisers from other agencies for adult education, also helps to place the institute in its true context. And that is salutary for everyone. For, if there is one danger in being part of an active evening institute, as organiser or teacher, it is that you may come to regard the institute as self-sufficient. Often, the principal is more prone to this feeling than anyone else. Like some teachers with their classes, he can begin to think that there can be very little wrong if people continue to come and his enrolments from year to year show no serious decline. But then, the people who come may have no other centre to go to; or, at least, no other centre that is different enough to offer them a meaningful choice.

Behind all this – the regular exchange of views between teachers and organisers, the local training courses and the regional training schemes – there is, of course, the contribution which the institute's own common room can make in developing a sense of community involvement for the teacher. Few institutes have their own staff rooms but, in any case, the general common room, which everyone can use, is invariably the best place for personal contacts. Furnished with comfortable chairs, a refreshment bar, a bookshelf for recent publications, a well-filled magazine rack and plenty of wallboards for displaying work, announcing projects and advertising local events, the common room offers an ideal meeting ground. Often enough, it is in that kind of environment that conversation begins to reveal the people behind the image of 'the organiser' and 'the teacher' and to stimulate discussion of a problem or a new way of doing things which shows how closely connected their different jobs are, and need to be.

In one such conversation a teacher said to me, 'You know, I've enjoyed this dressmaking class but next year I really would like to take a course that is a bit more advanced. The trouble is, if we call it "advanced" some of the people who ought to come to it might think it's too difficult for them.' Our discussion led us to think that the course might be centred on a project which would be attractive enough in itself but could involve advanced processes. It might be, for example, to make not just a dress but a complete outfit, and this would make it possible to include Millinery and Glove-making and to deal in a really effective way with colour and design and the choice of materials. Several teachers would be needed to work with a group like this: would there be too many administrative problems? We concluded, happily enough, that if there were going to be difficulties of that kind, then the way in which we administered our courses would have to be changed.

Relations between the institute and its students depend, first of all, quite naturally, on the degree of satisfaction and the sense of development and achievement which they get from the courses they have joined. But there are many ways in which, outside the classroom, the institute can influence a student's attitude to adult education and extend its usefulness to him. A good common room in which he can read and relax and talk – for a whole evening if he wants to; joint activities which break down some of the unnecessary barriers between classes and subjects; a notice-board which keeps him in touch with neighbourhood events: all these help him to feel part of a unit that is larger than his own class and encourage in him a wider view of his own capabilities.

The institute, in turn, derives its own benefits from that. For, the idea of membership of it, rather than membership, simply, of one or other of its classes, produces relationships through which students can, naturally and usefully, influence decisions about organisation and programme planning. Without that influence, some of those decisions may well be based on assumptions which are not really valid, and may lead to the offering of courses and activities which turn out to be irrelevant to actual needs.

Some organisers prefer to formalise these relationships and make them more explicit. In the past few years, for example, many centres and institutes across the country have introduced forms of organised student participation. Most of them provide for actual membership of the institute by students and for the election, by members, of student committees to help in management and planning. Other centres go much farther than this, handing over the initiative for what is done to local groups and voluntary societies. Others again, and perhaps they are the majority, would hold that the kind of student participation we need in adult education can only be encouraged through the quite informal, day-to-day relationships in which the teachers, the students and the organising staff of a well-run institute are naturally involved. And some would add that the danger of having formal committees for students is that the teacher may not be there when decisions are made to which he can contribute in a useful way.

My own view is that the rather special relationship of teacher and student in adult education, which derives, quite simply, from the student's adult experience and status, is one which can and ought to be extended outside the classroom; and that, if this is to be done effectively, formal student committees of one kind or another are needed. Moreover, the clear, outward recognition that the adult students of an institute have a part to play in influencing and guiding its development not only helps to establish its connections with the wider adult community around it, but also enables those connections to be made with meaning and good sense.

It is important for an institute to know about the needs of the neighbourhood it serves and to provide for them when it can. It will want to develop relations with local organisations providing educational and community services – community associations, youth clubs, music societies, art clubs, drama groups, and so on. A room may be found for the regular meetings of a local group, or the institute may offer the occasional use of a hall or an exhibition space or provide a course especially designed for a voluntary society and its members. That kind of help extends the influence of the institute's attitudes and values in education and does much to condition a healthy local response to its work as a whole. And a widely representative student committee can help to ensure that these links are made in the right way and when they are needed.

Secondly, if it decides, as many institutes do, from time to time, that it would like to offer affiliation to a particular local organisation – a branch of the W.E.A. for example – then its offer of that additional link, and the purpose behind it, can be immeasurably strengthened by giving the affiliated group a voice on the student committee.

There is, after all, no reason to suppose that teacher involvement and student participation cannot both work. Whether they take shape in formal committees or by *ad hoc* consultation will be, largely, a matter of local attitudes, traditions and needs. But to see that they do work, in one way or another is, as I have indicated, something which most organisers would regard as crucial to the job they have to do.

In this chapter I have tried to describe the work of one kind of organiser in adult education – the institute principal or the area organiser employed by a local education authority. In some ways this work is much the same as that of an organiser in a university Extra-Mural department, or a W.E.A. district or an independent centre for adult education. In other ways it is quite different. There are, of course, some differences in philosophy and attitude. In the main, however, the differences are quite practical ones deriving from the kinds of courses provided and the methods of teaching and organising which they demand. Present developments indicate that the various agencies for adult education may be able in future to work a good deal more closely together. And that would be helpful to organisers and teachers generally, for we have much to learn from each other.

Further reading

Teacher training and adult education in *Adult Education* Vol. 38, no. 6, March 1966, pp. 380–90 (Part 3 of an Appendix).

JONES, H. A. The centre idea – student participation in *Adult Education* Vol. 39, no. 4, Nov. 1966.

NATIONAL INSTITUTE OF ADULT EDUCATION
    Adult Education in 1968 The Inst., 1968, 10s. 6d.
    Adult Education in 1967 The Inst., 1967, 10s.

EDUCATIONAL TECHNOLOGY
by Leslie Ryder

Teaching aids need not be expensive or difficult to operate, but more important, adult students have a right to expect to see and use in the classroom the familiar domestic equipment of cameras, projectors, radio and television. Leslie Ryder, Aural and Visual Aids Inspector of the Inner London Education Authority, discusses in this chapter what help educational technology can and should bring to learner and teacher.

My first memory of wireless is of a large dark brown metal box, the top of which had to be removed if you wanted to change the station. Once the box was opened, the change was effected by pulling out two large coils and replacing them by others of a different colour. We had two sets, a yellow set and a purple set, and the one not in use lay carefully protected in a box on top of the wireless. Every Wednesday afternoon I used feverishly to try to substitute the purple coils for the yellow ones so that I could listen to Henry Hall and follow the musical saga of 'Rusty and Dusty Brown'. All this happened in south Cheshire in a black-and-white farmhouse lit by paraffin lamps.

Today we have three radios, and one of them is a VHF transistorised battery-operated portable. It is about 9 in. square and gives superb reception wherever we put it down. It has an extension socket for a tape recorder and simple yet sophisticated controls which my two small sons operate with ease. They take it for granted just as they do the radio in the car.

These developments in the provision of radio reception facilities have been paralleled by advances in all other forms of communication. Increased efficiency, ease of operation, portability, miniaturisation and, incidentally, a reduction in relative price have characterised developments in gramophones, tape recorders, cameras, film and slide projectors and more recently television sets and even videotape recorders. Just as today we have three radios, a gramophone and a tape recorder in my home, so in a few years time we can expect to have more than one television set and a videotape recorder.

Our society has asked for virtually instantaneous world coverage of news and entertainment, and that these be provided in our homes through a variety of communication media – print, sound, pictures, sound plus pictures. We have also asked that facilities be available whereby we can record and play back these sounds and pictures and even originate them ourselves.

As educationalists we must not ignore the fact that the vivid, immediate and highly professional presentation of ideas and experience available in the home may cause changes in the expectations which students bring to classes. We must not be surprised if they become dissatisfied with the dry-as-dust textbook or the average lecture. As G. Seldes writes in his book *The Great Audience* – 'The effect of the public arts cannot be escaped by turning off the radio or the television set – neither our indifference nor contempt gives us immunity against them.' Education which had made possible the great advances in communication techniques has remained somewhat aloof from their consequences and Marshal McLuhan suggests that when a child enters the normal school classroom he takes a step back in time. Compared with the communication facilities in the home, those of the school are medieval. If this is true for the secondary school child it is equally applicable to all levels of education including adult education.

Where we have a group of 20 well-motivated students, all of comparable ability, all pursuing the same course of study using the same materials in a fixed sequence and all proceeding at roughly the same pace, then we need provide nothing beyond a space for 20 seats, 20 texts and a teacher. The teacher may expound upon the informational context of the course, he will dictate the pace, and refer the students to the printed text. Only occasionally will there be any need for additional resources such as film, records, television and provision for these need not concern the educational providers. They are peripheral to the main teaching situation. To dispense with them causes no loss to teacher or taught. In this way audio-visual material has come to be regarded as a fill-in luxury, as an aid to the teacher where the word 'aid' is synonomous with 'first-aid' – something you hope to manage without, a step taken only in emergency. Even today one still hears the phrase 'Oh she's such a brilliant teacher, she needs no aids to help her'. One is delighted to encounter such living, walking, talking multi-media people and pleased to know they need no help in teaching, but what of their students, what kind of help do they need in learning? There may have been lots of responses in the lesson period, but as Professor Doris Lee points out in her paper, *Perception, Intuition and Insight*, the production of a response does not in itself guarantee meaning. As teachers we may feel we have taught well, but have our students learned well?

In a print-dominated education the student's ability to respond to a learning situation will depend upon his ability to respond to the written word. No matter how great his motivation or intellectual curiosity his response will be determined by his verbal skills. Words can only be interpreted in the light of previous experience and linguistic poverty may handicap more people than we realise. I sometimes wonder if as teachers we are always aware of the difficulties many students experience when faced with a page of print. I remember listening to a broadcast of 'Dr Zhivago' with a group of craft apprentices. After the broadcast there followed a discussion on personal relationships, changes in social behaviour, increasing tolerance of moral laxity in times of war, which would have done credit to any Sixth Form. When I showed them a paperback copy of the book costing 5/– none was prepared even to consider buying it. After some time the reason was poignantly given by one of the young men, 'There's no point, I couldn't make sense of all that print'.

The new media of communication encourage a reappraisal of the position of print in education. In many homes they already provide large numbers of people with information, ideas, experience as rich and vivid as others gain from books. Facilities which are available in the home must surely be tried in education not as peripheral aids to teaching but as an integral part of the total learning environment. This is not to suggest that verbal skills are not essential to mental development. With all visual media words are necessary to direct attention, establish connections, give names to images, provide stress and pace. Dr J. Trenaman in his book *Communication and Comprehension* writes 'It may be supposed that television is also enlarging and enriching the field of visual reference. ... The sound medium and the printed word may conjure up equally powerful images in the mind of the listener or reader, but those images, in so far as they have visual forms, are compounded of impressions taken in through visual perception. In a sense, then, one could describe these two media as derivative, whereas television is constantly adding to this visual store. . . . But even when it is using its visual capacities to the full television must rely on language to communicate very much of the meaning of what is seen.'

The new media provide us with opportunities for bringing the real, the practical world into our work, and so a model, a picture, a piece of film or a television programme becomes an aid 'to set in train the right kind and quality of perceptions from which learning can take place.' (Professor Doris Lee.)

Up to now education has been provided with too little of the wrong kind of equipment. The cumbersome, complicated, massive equipment supplied to most institutions often requires a safari team to move it and more often than not a divine inspiration to find it. Seldom does anyone cherish it and so its performance deteriorates until it ends up dust-covered in an unused cupboard. If anyone does look after it, then they are liable to become very possessive about it, putting it under permanent guard and defying anyone else to use it. 'The last time I lent it out, it was returned broken.' Neither the equipment nor its provision has in the past encouraged utilisation.

Today the development in what is called 'the hardware' seems to have polarised at two ends of a scale. On the one hand equipment is available to facilitate self-instruction and individual study – teaching machines, loop projectors, language laboratories, synchronised slides and tape. On the other hand are devices to facilitate mass teaching; film, television, radio and, in a single institution, the overhead projector, are means whereby the skills of a single teacher can be made available to large numbers of students.

For the first time we can therefore start to operate on two fronts ourselves. On the one hand we can examine ways in which we use our teaching talents; we can if we wish break down the isolation of most teaching situations and work as a team with our colleagues. Using the new equipment we can certainly share materials and we can take a critical look at the efficiency and effectiveness of our own communications. On the other hand we can provide a wide range of materials on which individual students can work. We can give them books and duplicated texts; we can let them listen to tapes and use the tape to improve a language drill. We can let them improve their own manipulative skills in craft or embroidery by letting them work with a continuous loop projector. We can provide them with a slide/tape constructional kit to fill in gaps in their understanding. With all these devices they can work at their own pace, they can be actively involved, they receive and make a response. And they can come to us for those aspects of education which no machine can provide – the discussion, the question and answer, the interplay of mind against mind. Indeed if we will allow machines to dispense some of the information then we may have more time for our teaching to become 'the joint enterprise of a group of friendly human beings to enjoy using their brains'. (Professor G. Highet, *The Art of Teaching*.) The new approaches to the use of audio-visual media ask to be thought out in detail. There is little to be gained if they merely decorate our existing teaching methods.

'Teach by doing whenever you can and only fall back on words when doing is out of the question.' So wrote Rousseau in *Émile* and today 'learning by doing' is a commonplace of pedagogy, but new educational techniques are influenced by the findings of modern psychology. The work of Professor Skinner stresses the importance of reward in the learning situation and has provided the basis of programmed learning. That of Professor Piaget emphasises not only the importance of the learner's needs, but also his 'readiness' or 'motivation' for the demands the learning will make upon him. Many young people and adults experience a depressing sense of failure because they are brought into contact with courses of study whose rigour is in advance of motivation. However, as Helen Coppen writes in her book, *Aids to Teaching and Learning*, 'Whatever the theorists say it is clear that teachers must present students with things to perceive, must help them to organise these precepts with schema or structures and that what they have retained or understood must be restated by the learner'.

This immediately raises the question of what things should our students be asked to perceive. In courses such as 'Flower Arrangement for beginners', 'You and the Law', 'Brush up your German' or 'Organising a Play Group' what are the aims of the teaching? The use of modern educational technology depends upon a definition of the objectives, long term and short term, of any course. Is 'Flower Arranging' the acquisition of a dubious artefact? Is 'You and the Law' a quick canter through the *Everyman's Guide*? How much of 'Brush up your German' involves a knowledge of grammar rather than fluent communication in the language? How detailed is the study of child development in the 'play group' course? These are the kinds of questions to be answered before a TV series, a film or a programmed text is even thought of, for there is evidence to suggest that much student learning failure stems from the teacher's failure to articulate learning objectives.

In her book, *Psychology, the starting point for educational reform,* Professor Doris Lee remarks that 'the craft of teaching has long been regarded as an intuitive dualism between teacher-presented material and selected learner acceptance'. Educational technology emphasises the importance of learning objectives and the assessment of results, and in so doing hopes to provide a more scientific basis on which to examine both the content and the methods of our teaching. It may prove a useful antidote to the inspired guesswork which characterises a lot of educational activity.

Some objectives may defy definition, and with others it is difficult to prove that they have been achieved, but the habit of thinking about them is important, for it leads to more carefully prepared material, and more purposeful activities on the part of the students. Every teacher needs to be an opportunist, but waiting for opportunities may result in the pursuit of 'red herrings' and time-wasting futilities, and in adult education the gradual disappearance of the class.

Once the objectives of the class have been decided, and it must be remembered that this is often a long and agonising process which cannot easily be carried out alone, then the teachers involved can begin to examine the ways in which these objectives can be achieved: the kinds of materials the student will need to use, the ways in which ideas are to be presented, the times when the teacher must demonstrate, the times when the students work on their own, the times when a teacher with a small group discusses or examines a topic. It is here that a whole new range of resources is now available. All this implies a wealth of resources and material on hand in the situation concerned, and these whether they be tape recorder and tape, loop projectors and 8 mm film cassettes, slide viewers and slides must be available with easy access for both teachers and students. If the new facilities are to be anything more than the odd additional tool for the teacher then more money has to be spent on them. The library has to extend its provision to include the storage and retrieval of all kinds of resources – abstracts, artefacts, tapes, slides, records, film so that students are referred to them as naturally as they are now referred to print.

With such facilities we can start to think about multi-media teaching, the integration of a variety of appropriate aids to gain the maximum learning and should all this seem something of a pious hope it is worth examining what is available so far.

For years the BBC has produced pamphlets to support its radio and television series and has now even in Adult Education started to provide transparencies for an Art series (*Rembrandt*) on radio. Records are now regarded as an integral part of television language courses and for its schools series in Mathematics and Physics 8 mm film loops are available. Series such as *Man* on radio and the Primary school *Religious Service* have provided large charts for classroom use. Already multi-media materials are available and the variety from a broadcasting organisation alone is considerable. Today no self-respecting publisher would produce a language textbook without supporting tape recordings. All these are sound developments. The diversity of our students, their different backgrounds, experiences, vocabulary, and interests would indicate the need for variety in the presentation of ideas and experience. The greater this variety, the more likely it is that we shall be able to meet their individual learning needs and retain their continuing interest.

Without interest and a desire to learn no progress is, of course, possible, but in adult education classes motivation must be considerable. The students have come of their own volition, they are even prepared to pay for what is to be provided. As Professor Jones has pointed out earlier, their expectations must be high. Having examined our course, assembled the materials for a variety of situations and planned a line of action we must not forget to ask ourselves why the students have come, what hopes they have of the course. Our first duty is to get to know them, and this will immediately alert us to the differences that exist. In a 'Dressmaking' or 'Woodworking' class there will be those who already possess a knowledge of the materials, others who have limited skills and yet others for whom the simple act of measuring accurately is a major challenge. How do we cope with these varying levels ? Do our students wait until we get round to them before they can start to work ? Are they expected to pick up what they can from others ? Do we press forward without ever checking their learning ? In these situations a variety of learning materials is necessary so that students can work at their own pace and measure their own success. We provide the real materials so that through tactile and sensory experience students can assess their special qualities and textures and we provide slides showing the materials made up. We demonstrate a manipulative skill, but when do we stop ? How do we know that students have grasped the technique ? Rather than letting them fumble through, could we have an 8 mm cassetted film loop which shows the skills over and over again from the view-point of the operator ? Using this by himself the student could practise until he felt confident. Is there a programmed text which would help the student with his mathematical difficulties ? Once the skills have been mastered on the object created what do we provide as extension of this experience ? What of the operation of design ? Do we discuss it at all and, if so, what common experiences do we provide as a start-ing point for the discussion – sets of pictures, a film, a television programme ?

The range of opportunities in Dressmaking or Woodwork is avail-able for Sociology, for library study, for language teaching, for Art, indeed for anything we care to mention.

Educational technology then is not a teacher coming into a class-room weighed down with hardware, nor is it a student spending all his time watching television or with earphones and a tape recorder. It is teachers examining the way they teach, defining the content of their courses and then selecting the best materials to achieve those ends with the students who are working with them.

Further reading

ATKINSON, N. J. *Modern teaching aids* Maclaren, 1966.

COPPEN, H. E. *Aids to teaching and learning* Pergamon P., 1969.

ERICKSON, C. W. H. *Fundamentals of teaching with audio-visual technology* Collier-Macmillan, 1965.

RICHMOND, W. K. *Teachers and machines* Collins, 1965.

THOMAS, R. M. and SWARTOUT, S. G. *Integrated teaching materials: how to choose, create and use them* New York: Longmans, 1960.

The National Committee for Audio Visual Aids in Education publishes a wide range of guides on specific aural and visual aids, e.g. '8 mm in Education', 'Guide for the production of wall charts', 'Choosing a tape recorder', 'The Overhead Projector', etc. Details can be obtained from 33 Queen Anne Street, London, W.1.

Some Catalogues and useful addresses

British National Film Catalogue (published six times per year), 193/197 Regent Street, London, W.1.

Catalogue of 8 mm Cassette Films, Educational Foundation for Visual Aids, 33 Queen Anne Street, London, W.1.

Visual Aids: Film Strips and Films, Pts. 1–8 (revised every alternate year), Educational Foundation for Visual Aids, 33 Queen Anne Street, London, W.1.

British Film Institute and Society for Education in Film and Television, both at 81 Dean Street, London, W.1.

National Audio-Visual Aids Centre, Paxton Place, Gipsy Road, London, S.E.27.

OUTSIDE HELP
by Derek Buchanan

Names, addresses and information on where the part-time teacher can find outside help and support, compiled by Derek Buchanan, Deputy Secretary of the National Institute for Adult Education.

Support and encouragement comes from sharing your problems and finding that others have very similar ones. Exchange class visits with another tutor and criticise each other's methods. There are a number of supporting organisations available, among which the:

Association for Adult Education is mainly for principals and organisers;

Association of Teachers in Technical Institutions is mainly for teachers in colleges of further education and art colleges;

National Federation of Continuative Teachers Association is for those teaching similar, mainly practical, subjects in adult centres and institutes;

Association of Tutors in Adult Education is mainly for university and W.E.A. tutors;

Association for Liberal Education unites those whose work is to widen the education of vocational students in local authority colleges.

These organisations are not necessarily established in all areas, but will welcome enquiries. Many areas have already thriving teachers centres, some conceived entirely as short-course centres and libraries of teaching aids, others including a social purpose as well. Although this intention is primarily for the day-school teacher, your education office will be quite likely to encourage enthusiastic part-time teachers to use its facilities.

The Educational Centres Association has a number of national and regional conferences for members and staff of those adult centres which encourage student participation in more than the classroom activity, and see the value of joining the E.C.A.

Your Local Authority will sometimes provide courses for part-time teachers, and will often receive details of courses offered by the Department of Education and Science, Universities and other local authorities. Training opportunities have developed relatively rapidly in recent years, and some authorities are willing to second teachers to the university diploma courses, some of them part-time, recently established at Manchester, Nottingham, Hull, Edinburgh and Glasgow. It is up to you to make sure that your principal and education office know of your interest in courses.

Remember also that the public programmes of your nearest university's Extra-Mural department, W.E.A. branch, or L.E.A. evening centre offer a wide range of possibilities for the part-time teacher concerned to extend his own education beyond his particular specialisation.

For those with a knowledge of languages, the European Bureau of Adult Education keeps open the contact with similar work going on in other countries, arranging conferences and meetings, and publishing *Notes and Studies*.

The magazine most immediate to the part-time teacher of practical subjects is *Teaching Adults*, whilst *Adult Education* is a more substantial journal for those whose primary concern is with the practice and situation of adult education. There are of course items of value to all practitioners in both. These are published by the National Institute of Adult Education, which also publishes pamphlets from time to time, many of them of great interest to part-time teachers. *Dialogue* published by the Schools Council is an easily read digest of the most recent research on educational methods, *Visual Education* an excellent promoter of education aids. *Studies in Adult Education*, first issued in April 1969, contains more substantial articles. A fuller list is appended.

The BBC produces a large amount of publicity for specific further education programmes, and is anxious to encourage the use of this in groups; the ITA also offers a small number of courses. Day-time educational radio also provides excellent material which you can either tape for your class, or direct members to hear or see at home as reinforcement of, or preparation for, classwork.

The weekly educational journals could with advantage reflect more of the work going forward with adults, and workers in adult education should relate their work to the wider field of education.

Your contributions to and support of all these publications and associations increase the impact of adult education on the community, and so work directly and indirectly for a better service.

Associations

For Adult Education, 28 Greenhanger Avenue, Benstead, Surrey
of Tutors in Technical Institutions, Hamilton House, Mabledon Place, London, W.C.1
of Tutors in Adult Education, 1066 Green Lane, Temple Ewell, Kent
for Liberal Education, Stuart House, Mill Lane, Cambridge
National Federation of Continuative Teachers, 44 Trinity Church Square, Trinity Street, London, S.E.1
Educational Centres, Greenleaf Road, London, E.17

Other course providers

Department of Education and Science, Elizabeth House, 29 York Road, London, S.E.1
National Institute of Adult Education, 35 Queen Anne Street, London, W1M OBL
BBC, Broadcasting House, London W1A 1AA.

Publications

Teaching Adults, National Institute of Adult Education
Adult Education, National Institute of Adult Education
Studies in Adult Education, Universities Council for Adult Education, 9 Abercromby Square, Liverpool 7
Notes and Studies, Huize 'Krankenburgh' Hoflaan 22, Bergen (NH) Netherlands
Convergence, P.O. Box 250, Station 'F', Toronto 5, Ontario, Canada
W.E.A. News, Temple House, 9 Upper Berkeley Street, London, W.1
Liberal Education, Association for Liberal Education
Vocational Aspects of Secondary and Further Education, Pergamon Press, Oxford
Trends in Education, Department of Education and Science
New University, 22 Grays Inn Road, London, W.C.1
Visual Education, 33 Queen Anne Street, London W1M OBL
Dialogue, Schools Council, 160 Great Portland Street, London, W1N 5TB
Where ? Advisory Centre for Education, 57 Russell Street, Cambridge
Times Educational Supplement, Printing House Square, London, E.C.4
Education, 10 Queen Anne Street, London, W.1

TV AND THE TRAINING OF ADULT TEACHERS

by Jennifer Rogers

All the chapters in this book have grown out of the original BBC series 'Teaching Adults'. Some of the authors appeared as contributors in the series, all of them have written their chapters as a result of some vein of interest which the series seemed to provoke. This chapter describes what 'Teaching Adults' set out to do, and some of the effects it had. The author is BBC Further Education Officer for the south of England.

There were many people who thought that 'Teaching Adults' couldn't be done. Adult education, they thought, was too diffuse a world to bear the prolonged and steady scrutiny of a ten-programme television series. Were there really enough links between the skills needed by an Industrial Training Officer, an Extra-Mural tutor in philosophy and a soft-furnishings tutor at an Evening Institute? These were honest and real enough misgivings, but advice from both policy-makers and practitioners in adult education suggested strongly not only that there was a good deal in common between these apparently diverse worlds but also that there was a real training job to do and that television could help do it.

It was against this background that Roger Owen, the producer, and Anthony Cash, his director, started to plan their series. Obviously there would be little point in dissecting the Adult Education world itself; this was to be a series about teaching adults, not about Adult Education, with all the portentousness that the capital letters usually imply. The series was to aim at giving solid, practical advice to teachers of adults, many of whom are enthusiastic subject specialists but untrained teachers, or else are trained to cope with children during the day, but unskilled or uncertain about how to adapt their teaching techniques to their adult evening class. The series would attempt to show from recent research into learning how adults differ from children in the classroom, and would follow this up by a variety of filmed 'real' classroom situations and studio demonstrations. The formula was a fruitful one. It worked out in practice to ten programmes on these subjects and in this order:

The students – who they are and why they come; the organizers; two programmes on theoretical and practical aspects of adults as learners; 'extending the subject'; teaching in the Army; lecturing techniques; project methods; relationships in the group; and a final programme called 'Survey' which summarised the themes of the series.*

Whatever timing a programme has, it will always be inconvenient for some people. The Sunday morning timing, particularly, was felt to be a severe challenge by many viewers who were anxious to make it clear to us that getting up in time to watch the programme at 9.30 a.m. on a Sunday was an unparalleled feat of virtue and heroism on their part. The repeat the following Saturday was probably a 'better' time for many people, and was, of course, the one chosen by the study groups who met to follow the programmes together.

This part of our regular 100,000 audience was at least easy to track down, and in some ways easy to cater for. From the start, the series was planned on the assumption that study groups would be organised, as previous forays in linked television and study group learning have shown how successful such methods can be (e.g. 'The Social Workers', 'The Supervisors' and many other further education series). The series was announced in our Further Education Advance Information leaflet; anyone who later indicated that they were interested in forming a group was invited to write in for free copies of notes on the programme for group tutors.

These tutors' notes proved highly satisfactory to most of those who used them and were widely praised for 'giving a clear indication of the producer's intentions', and most important, for the 'helpful, detailed and practical' suggestions they contained on conducting the post-programme discussion. As is usual in tutors' notes these suggested 'leaders' for discussion topics were made with some diffidence; it was made clear that they really were suggestions only and that many groups might prefer to develop their discussion out of their own needs and interests. It is intriguing then, that so many groups grasped eagerly at the suggested discussion topics, and when later writing up

* The programmes went out weekly between 21 April and 29 June 1968 on Sundays on BBC-1 at 9.30 a.m. with a repeat the following Saturday at 10.30 a.m. Because most teaching of adults goes on in the evening we hoped that this weekend transmission-time would give opportunities for watching the programme to anyone who was interested. The series is repeated on Thursdays on BBC-2, 7.00–7.30 p.m. from 9 October to 11 December 1969.

their opinions of the whole exercise for our questionnaire gave the tutors' notes a special mention for usefulness. It suggests, perhaps, that for study groups of this kind which usually meet only for the duration of the series, group leaders feel unusually vulnerable and are frankly glad to have detailed suggestions for follow-up activity.

Something like 200 groups, involving perhaps 2,000 people, were eventually recruited. The details of course arrangements were, naturally, left to the course organisers, and it was soon clear that the series was proving to have a very wide appeal. The majority of groups came from the L.E.A. Evening Institutes, but several dozen were formed by University Extra-Mural departments or W.E.A. tutors. There were groups of clergymen, groups of youth leaders, army officers, even a group of sister-tutors from a large teaching hospital. The average size of each group was ten, but we know of one enormous group of over 80 which met and flourished every Saturday morning in Bristol, and there were several other large groups where over 30 teachers attended faithfully. Once started, it was a measure of the interest created by the programmes that only a tiny number of groups collapsed, mostly because recruitment was initially too small to sustain good discussion. One group had to stop, intriguingly, because of 'emergency archaeological excavations on city walls'.

People who watch television programmes in groups, and as part of a training exercise, have very different needs, and make a formidably different audience from those who watch singly and snugly in their own armchairs. The armchair viewer is satisfied generally by a meaty, but rounded-off programme. It is more irritating to be enticed and teased by loose ends in an argument when you can only thunder your discontent at your family. On the other hand, the study group audience wants, and can take, something harder to handle. For instance, although study groups generally agree that the 'expert' has his place in a programme, they usually feel impatient if experts are wheeled on so often that there is too little time for film of real classroom teaching. Study groups demand loose ends, they want to feel they can take the argument further themselves so that they can adapt it to their own particular needs. Not only that, the member of a study group is instantly put on his mettle by knowing he is going to discuss the programme after it has finished, and watches it therefore with an altogether more critical eye than he might do at home.

The differences between these two types of audience show startlingly in the two sorts of questionnaires we distributed after the series finished. Questionnaires distributed initially through the National Institute for Adult Education journal *Adult Education* were filled in largely by people watching at home. They had criticisms, of course, but they also gave clear and firm approval to almost every programme. In a space on the questionnaire for 'disappointing features of the programme', a very large number of people wrote 'None'.

On the other hand, many people watching in study groups tended to say as this L.E.A. Course organiser did on a second questionnaire sent to study group tutors: 'These programmes have been really excellent, particularly as they have given us opportunities to see other teachers at work. But what we value very highly indeed is our discussions afterwards where we have taken things very much more deeply than you could. Naturally, we also have to remember that without the BBC, we wouldn't have had the discussions!'

There was no need for group tutors to feel apologetic about the high standards of their discussions. The programmes were never meant to be a complete guide to everything that could be said about teaching adults – they were meant to stimulate thought and discussion, and in places they were meant to be controversial. In this they certainly succeeded. In my own visits to study groups I listened to some hectic and noisy debates on whether or not a Principal should sit in on a teacher's class ('It's spying' – 'No, no, it's *training*') on the 'discovery' method described in the series, as in this book, by Dr Belbin, and on the merits and demerits of inviting an outside visitor into the classroom. The discovery method, and the kind of active, participatory learning it invites was hotly debated everywhere. I remember with pleasure one or two powerful and absorbing discussions where group members worked out exactly how and how far discovery methods could be applied to their work. Some people in other study groups felt we had oversold 'discovery' learning in the series; one history tutor tartly commented to me, 'What am I supposed to do – lay on the Battle of Waterloo in Parliament Hill Fields?' But then an equal number of people seemed to feel that discovery learning was still new enough to need plenty of emphasis; as one returned questionnaire bluntly put it, 'You can't say it loud enough or long enough because most of my teachers still think that all they've got to do is get up on their hind legs and talk for two hours'.

Undoubtedly, most of our audience, at home or in study groups, felt that the most interesting and valuable parts of the series were the opportunities to see other teachers at work. Teaching is a lonely profession. You rarely see other teachers teaching. You can rarely measure your own abilities with theirs. Television can obviously do a useful job here. Some teachers reacted jealously, or over-confidently at the pieces of film we used – 'I can do better than that'. But the majority felt reassured that they were on the right lines, or else simply enjoyed and admired another teacher's expertise, whether it was in demonstrating simple industrial skills or in teaching a basic design course. A very few study group members refused to be shifted from their erroneous belief that classroom sessions and studio demonstrations alike had been 'faked' or 'rehearsed'. This accusation must be taken as a form of compliment to the producer's skill.

Apart from weekly study groups, we know of at least ten colleges and Institutes which asked teachers to watch the programmes at home in preparation for one grand conference at the end. The series also seems to have entered the mainstream of available material on teaching adults and to have become a constant point of reference for conferences and training schemes since it ended and, of course, the life of the series is being prolonged by its BBC-2 repeat in autumn 1969 and by this book, where many of the contributors have been invited to extend and amplify statements they originally made in 'Teaching Adults'.

Some of the groups which formed during the series did so out of sheer interest, but the motive behind the formation of most of them seems to have been a wish to embark on a perfectly serious but informal training programme with the television series as its centre. We know that some local authorities were sceptical about whether it was possible to train part-time teachers of adults at all, because part-time teachers are popularly supposed to carry their teaching responsibilities lightly.

Response to the series quickly proved them wrong. The teachers did enrol, they came to courses lasting ten consecutive Saturday mornings and we hoped they felt they had learnt something – most of them certainly enjoyed themselves. One Principal wrote, 'We have all so much enjoyed meeting each other regularly that our group has acquired a social as well as an academic impetus. We only wish we'd thought of doing something similar much earlier ourselves. . . .'

Further reading

NATIONAL INSTITUTE OF ADULT EDUCATION AND UNESCO *Adult education and television: a comparative study in Canada, Czechoslovakia and Japan*; ed. by B. Groombridge. The Inst., 1966.

MOIR, G., ed. *Teaching and television: E.T.V. explained* Pergamon P., 1967.

NATIONAL INSTITUTE OF ADULT EDUCATION *Teaching through television*; by H. Wiltshire and F. Bayliss. The Inst., 1965.

NATIONAL INSTITUTE OF ADULT EDUCATION *Television and social work*; by A. Hancock and J. Robinson. The Inst., 1966.

ROBINSON, J. and BARNES, N., eds. *New media and methods in industrial training* BBC, 1968.

ROBINSON, J., ed. *Educational television and radio in Britain* BBC, 1966.